CW00543938

In the Jaws of the
CROCODILE

In the Jaws of the
CROCODILE

EMMERSON MNANGAGWA'S RISE TO POWER IN ZIMBABWE

RAY NDLOVU

PENGUIN BOOKS

Published by Penguin Books
an imprint of·Penguin Random House South Africa (Pty) Ltd
Reg. No. 1953/000441/07
The Estuaries No. 4, Oxbow Crescent, Century Avenue, Century City, 7441
PO Box 1144, Cape Town, 8000, South Africa
www.penguinrandomhouse.co.za

Penguin
Random House
South Africa

First published 2018

1 3 5 7 9 10 8 6 4 2

Publication © Penguin Random House 2018
Text © Ray Ndlovu 2018

All rights reserved. No part of this publication may be reproduced,
stored in a retrieval system or transmitted, in any form or by any means,
electronic, mechanical, photocopying, recording or otherwise,
without the prior written permission of the copyright owners.

PUBLISHER: Marlene Fryer
MANAGING EDITOR: Robert Plummer
EDITOR: Russell Martin
PROOFREADER: Dane Wallace
COVER AND TEXT DESIGNER: Ryan Africa
TYPESETTER: Monique van den Berg
INDEXER: Sanet le Roux

Set in 11.5 pt on 16 pt Minion

Printed by **novus print**, a Novus Holdings company

Penguin Random House is committed to a sustainable future for
our business, our readers and our planet. This book is made
from Forest Stewardship Council® certified paper.

ISBN 978 1 77609 348 9 (print)
ISBN 978 1 77609 349 6 (ePub)

Dedicated to
Yvonne Valerie Monica Ndlovu, my wife, for the best part of every day, and to Zoë Grace Ndlovu, our daughter, a daily source of joy.

Contents

Foreword

Emmerson Dambudzo Mnangagwa became the new president of Zimbabwe after the dramatic events of November 2017 that ended when Robert Mugabe shamefully resigned from office after thirty-seven years in power.

Mnangagwa's rise to the presidency after years of waiting on the sidelines was remarkable. More often than not, it seemed during those years that the presidency would elude him. Mugabe would not name a successor, nor would Nature take him to the other side. In November 2017, when Mnangagwa was fired as vice-president, it briefly seemed that the First Lady, Grace Mugabe, was on the cusp of succeeding her husband, and that Mnangagwa would be denied the country's top position for the umpteenth time.

In March 2018, together with the author of this book, I sat face to face with the man who had taken several decades to become president, just as he reached his first hundred-day mark in office. During the interview, Mnangagwa opened up about the serious challenges the country faced and the mess that his predecessor had bequeathed him. I was left with the impression that Mnangagwa does have a plan, a vision and the will to fix Zimbabwe. But, of course, whether he is going to make a difference and perform the skilful surgery that Zimbabwe needs is another story altogether.

The pain that Zimbabwe has gone through over the past few years is immense. At first glance it is easy to identify the toll that the years of misrule have taken on the economy of Zimbabwe, which once was the envy of many African nations. Yet that is a far too superficial analysis. It fails to consider the emotional pain and psychological scarring that Zimbabwe and its beautiful citizens have suffered.

Although an outsider, I identify with what Zimbabweans have experienced. I was banned from the country, before I had ever set foot in it, because I had exposed one of Mugabe's henchmen, the then minister of information, Jonathan Moyo, for going on a shopping spree in South Africa when Zimbabwe's own citizens were famished. When the Johannesburg *Sunday Times* published the story in January 2003, Moyo lost his temper. He said I was 'filthy and recklessly uncouth'. He went on to call me names, labelled me a spy and had me declared *persona non grata* in Zimbabwe.

So in November 2017 when I got the news that there was a power shift in Zimbabwe and that Moyo and company were on the run after their palatial homes had been raided by the army, I went to Zimbabwe for the first time, to witness the imminent downfall of Mugabe. It was a conscious decision, an almost revolutionary decision for me, as I did not care whether I was going to be arrested at the airport. I just wanted to be there when history was being made and the tyrant fell.

I landed in Harare at night. It seemed that the stars were smiling and I thought to myself that the gods were whispering '*tigamuchire mwana wevhu*', which means 'welcome, son of the soil'. No questions were asked and my passport was stamped, and I then proceeded to watch history unfold from the front lines.

The following morning I woke up to the people's march where victory chants and excitement in the streets were the order of the day. I joined the march, sang and danced to songs of freedom and victory, as the end was near. Old wounds were still fresh, but the tears of joy that flowed on the streets of Zimbabwe refreshed the hundreds of thousands of people who turned out to witness the dawn of a new era.

This book does more than just follow the rise of Mnangagwa to power. In essence, it captures the involvement in events of ordinary people who, when united by a common cause, can move seemingly impossible mountains before them and in the process write a glorious future for themselves. *In the Jaws of the Crocodile* is thus about much more than the power struggles in the ruling Zanu-PF party and the succession contest between Mnangagwa and other politicians that peaked in November 2017. It is about an entire nation's pain, anger and sense of betrayal at having their future stolen right before their eyes.

The Mugabe of November 2017 was a far cry from the man who had stepped onto the political stage as leader of a new and democratic Zimbabwe on 4 March 1980 and promised his people that Zimbabwe would be their land of milk and honey. 'Surely this is now time to beat our swords into ploughshares so we can attend to the problems of developing our economy and our society,' Mugabe had said.

But the early years of promise and high expectations at independence had given way over the years to power-mongering, ruthlessness and an insatiable appetite for power. The people of Zimbabwe were betrayed by a leader they had loved and trusted, and their patriotism was trodden upon or else taken for granted, all for the sake of self-enrichment.

It is a vital lesson for all generations to come that no single person can be more important than the people of a nation. As the new leader of Zimbabwe, Mnangagwa would do well to heed this lesson of his country's recent history.

MZILIKAZI WA AFRIKA
JOHANNESBURG, AUGUST 2018

Acknowledgements

The writing of this book would not have been possible without the contributions, guidance and assistance in different ways of the following people: Dr Delta Lau Milayo Ndou, you were my second pair of eyes. I am forever grateful for your immense patience and views throughout the writing of this book. Carien du Plessis, my friend who first nudged me to write about the events of November 2017. Thank you for your faith in me and believing that I could do this. Mzilikazi wa Afrika, the big brother I never had. The story of Zimbabwe's political transition is one that we saw and experienced together. I would never have done this without your help. You are an inspiration. Lenin Ndebele, thank you for your valuable insights and institutional knowledge. I cannot think of anyone who knows my journey, and all the struggles that came with it, more than you. Wilson Johwa, the news editor at *Business Day* who helped stretch my imagination. Bongani Siqoko, the *Sunday Times* editor, and Moshoeshoe Monare, deputy GM at Tiso Blackstar, thank you for entrusting me with the responsibility to 'own' and tell the Zimbabwe story. Ron Derby and Samantha Enslin-Payne, my editors at *Sunday Times Business Times*; thank you for giving me a chance when no one else would. A special mention to my *Business Times* colleagues; you all make work fun. Apostle Tavonga and Pastor Chipo Vutabwashe, thank you for your love and prayers. Takudzwa

Mafongoya, for the sound and measured advice you gave that helped keep my feet on the ground. Lastly, to my family: Edward Ndlovu, my dad, a bookworm; Anna Ndlovu, my mum, the single largest personal investor in my journalism career; Ayanda Ndlovu, my young brother and biggest fan; and Linda Ndlovu, my little sister and the baby of the family.

RAY NDLOVU
HARARE, AUGUST 2018

Timeline of key events in November 2017

- **4 November:** Zanu-PF holds a rally at White City Stadium, Bulawayo. Grace Mugabe is booed and President Robert Mugabe threatens to fire Vice-President Emmerson Mnangagwa.
- **5 November:** Grace Mugabe holds a rally at Rufaro Stadium in Harare with members of the Apostolic Church and calls for Mnangagwa's dismissal.
- **6 November:** Information minister Simon Khaya-Moyo announces that Mugabe has fired Mnangagwa as vice-president of Zimbabwe with immediate effect.
- **8 November:** Mnangagwa issues a statement in exile in which he says he will return in weeks and take over the running of the government and the party. He is fired from Zanu-PF, which holds a Politburo meeting and also begins a purge of Mnangagwa allies in the party.
- **12 November:** General Constantino Chiwenga, commander of the Zimbabwe Defence Forces, returns from China. An attempt is foiled to have him arrested by military personnel upon arrival at the airport in Harare.
- **13 November:** Chiwenga issues a statement and warns Zanu-PF to stop its internal purges, which are a source of instability for the nation.

- **14 November:** Kudzai Chipanga, the Zanu-PF Youth League chairperson, holds a press conference at the Zanu-PF headquarters in Harare. The Youth League is ready to die for Mugabe, he says, and he tells the army to stay in their barracks.
- Mugabe holds his last full cabinet meeting at the Munhumutapa offices in Harare.
- Army tanks are seen in the late afternoon leaving Inkomo Barracks and heading for Harare.
- Explosions and the sound of gunfire are heard in different parts of Harare that night.
- **15 November:** Major-General Sibusiso Moyo announces on the Zimbabwe Broadcasting Corporation at 4 a.m. that the army was carrying out an operation to target 'criminal elements' around Mugabe.
- South African president Jacob Zuma releases a statement and urges peace and calm in Zimbabwe. Zuma indicates that he has spoken to Mugabe, who is well but confined to his house.
- **16 November:** Zuma dispatches special envoys to Zimbabwe on behalf of the regional body, SADC, to establish what the situation is in Harare. Pictures are released by the media of Mugabe seated next to General Chiwenga at State House.
- **17 November:** The war veterans' chairperson, Christopher Mutsvangwa, returns from South Africa and holds a press briefing at an upmarket hotel. Mutsvangwa asks citizens to turn out in their numbers and participate in a march to call on Mugabe to step down.
- **18 November:** Hundreds of thousands of citizens take to the streets in Harare and Bulawayo.
- **19 November:** The Central Committee of Zanu-PF meets in Harare, and Mugabe is recalled as party leader. He is issued with a twenty-four-hour ultimatum to tender his resignation from office or risk impeachment. Grace Mugabe and several of her close allies, who include Jonathan Moyo, the higher education minister, are issued lifetime bans by Zanu-PF.

- At 9 p.m. Mugabe makes a televised speech to the nation flanked by army generals at State House. He absolves the generals of any wrongdoing and says he will preside over the Zanu-PF's elective congress to be held in December.
- **20 November:** The twenty-four-hour ultimatum handed to Mugabe by Zanu-PF lapses without any notice of resignation being tendered. Zanu-PF's chief whip informs the Speaker of Parliament that the party will institute an impeachment process against Mugabe.
- Mnangagwa issues a statement and urges Mugabe to listen to the people's wishes that he step down.
- **21 November:** A joint sitting of Parliament is held. Minutes before the impeachment vote is about to start, justice minister Happyton Bonyongwe hands over a letter to the Speaker of Parliament in which Mugabe resigns as the president of Zimbabwe.
- Jubilant scenes break out across Zimbabwe as news of Mugabe's resignation spreads.
- **22 November:** Mnangagwa returns from exile in South Africa to Harare under heavy military escort. He addresses party supporters outside the Zanu-PF headquarters at about 7 p.m.
- **24 November:** Mnangagwa is inaugurated as third president of the Republic of Zimbabwe at the National Sports Stadium. His inauguration is attended by several heads of state from the SADC region. Former colonial power Britain dispatches its top envoy to Africa, Rory Stewart, to attend the ceremony. Morgan Tsvangirai, the founding president of the opposition Movement for Democratic Change, is present as well.

Abbreviations

BBC: British Broadcasting Corporation
CBD: central business district
CIO: Central Intelligence Organisation
EU: European Union
MDC: Movement for Democratic Change
NRZ: National Railways of Zimbabwe
SADC: Southern African Development Community
Zanu: Zimbabwe African National Union
Zanu-PF: Zimbabwe African National Union – Patriotic Front
Zapu: Zimbabwe African People's Union
ZBC: Zimbabwe Broadcasting Corporation
ZDF: Zimbabwe Defence Forces
ZEC: Zimbabwe Electoral Commission

'I never expected that President Robert Mugabe would ever fire me, because in my view I had full loyalty towards him. I was committed to my party, committed to my government, committed and loyal to my leader to the end. I also believe that he knew that I was loyal to him and I would never ever do anything against him.'

– Emmerson Mnangagwa, in an exclusive interview in Harare, Zimbabwe, March 2018

Introduction

On 24 November 2017 Emmerson Dambudzo Mnangagwa became Zimbabwe's third president, replacing his mentor and long-time associate Robert Mugabe, who had shown no willingness to relinquish power after being at the helm of government for thirty-seven years. This was the culmination of a surreal and unimaginable period of twenty-one days in Zimbabwe's history. It all began when Mugabe fired Mnangagwa from his administration and from Zanu-PF, a few days after his wife, Grace Mugabe, had been booed and heckled at a rally in Bulawayo. At the time it seemed that Mugabe had ended Mnangagwa's long political career, along with his aspirations for high office. But as it turned out, the ninety-four-year-old president's victory was short-lived.

Drawing on a range of interviews with family members, senior figures in Zanu-PF and members of Mnangagwa's inner circle, *In the Jaws of the Crocodile* explores the behind-the-scenes story of how Mnangagwa overcame his setback and, in a matter of days, acceded to power in Zimbabwe.

From self-imposed exile in South Africa, where he had sought refuge after fearing for his life, Mnangagwa told Mugabe that he would return 'in a matter of weeks' to take control of the levers of power, both in government and in Zanu-PF. But this was a precarious journey in which success was far from certain. Family members, business associates and allies placed their lives at risk to assist him. The ties that Mnangagwa had forged in the Rhodesian Bush War of the late 1970s also bore fruit, as the military generals came out fighting in Mnangagwa's corner. Army tanks appeared on the streets and a senior officer announced on the national broadcaster that the army was carrying out an operation to remove 'criminal elements' around the president. Would this diverse array of supporters remain loyal or would they cave in under the immense pressure brought to bear on them at a time when Mnangagwa most needed their help?

Sensing a new dawn after the intervention by the military, Zimbabweans also came out in support. Large numbers of people in Harare and Bulawayo, containing their fear, ventured out into the streets to send an unequivocal message that Mugabe's days were over.

Mnangagwa's rapid rise to power, after years of speculation as to whether he was Mugabe's chosen successor, captured the national imagination. The implications of his ascent have reverberated beyond the country's borders, to the subregion and to the continent as a whole.

Could a new era finally have begun for Zimbabwe?

1

A turning point

Bulawayo is the second-largest city in Zimbabwe after Harare, the capital. Its name, loosely translated, means 'place of killing'. It was the seat of power of King Lobengula, the last Ndebele king, before his fall at the hands of the British pioneer column in the 1890s. Folklore has it that at the time of the establishment of the city, there was a civil war in which the young Lobengula was pitted against a group of Ndebele warriors who sought to block his rise as heir of Mzilikazi, his father. Given the resistance to his ascendancy, the prince named the capital 'KoBulawayo UmntwaneNkosi', which means 'the place where the prince is being killed'.

In the twentieth century, Bulawayo transformed itself from a city of bloodletting to the industrial hub of Zimbabwe. Colloquially, it is referred to as 'KoNtuthuziyathunqa', which means 'the place of smoke', a reference to the smoke that rises above its skyline from its many manufacturing industries. Parastatals such as the National Railways of Zimbabwe (NRZ) are also headquartered in the city, which enjoys close proximity to South Africa, the country's largest trading partner.

But since the year 2000, the city has been dealt a catastrophic blow by the economic collapse of Zimbabwe. Most of its inhabitants have migrated to South Africa and some to Harare, in search of greener pastures. So severe was the economic meltdown that companies that used to operate in Bulawayo have either shut down or relocated offices to Harare, in a last-ditch effort to remain afloat. In 2014, the Industry and Commerce Ministry estimated that about a hundred companies with operations in the city closed down. With very little economic activity taking place, President Robert Mugabe called Bulawayo an 'industrial scrap-yard' in his inauguration speech after the 2013 elections.

But besides being a ghost city afflicted by economic and industrial decay, Bulawayo is a city that has never fully embraced Zanu-PF. This is despite the Unity Accord of 1987 signed by Mugabe, as head of the Zimbabwe African National Union (Zanu), and the late nationalist leader Joshua Nkomo, head of the Zimbabwe African People's Union (Zapu), which led to Zapu's demise. Nkomo's party had once dominated politics in the city and in the rest of the Matabeleland region, and neither was ever fully won over to Zanu. Proof of Zanu-PF's failure to achieve comparable acceptance in the region can be illustrated by its poor showing in national elections in Matabeleland, especially since the emergence of the Movement for Democratic Change (MDC) in 2000, which gave voters an alternative they readily embraced. The Matabeleland region has since become the MDC's main stronghold.

Apart from the widespread loathing of Mugabe for his ruinous governance of the country, and the rejection of Zanu-PF in Matabeleland because of many grievances including economic and cultural marginalisation, it was the citizens in this part of the country who bore the brunt of the Gukurahundi campaign of the mid-1980s. Ostensibly this military campaign was targeted at armed 'dissidents', but in reality it was a form of genocide conducted against the country's predominantly Ndebele-speaking minority. For Mugabe and other Zanu-PF leaders, venturing into Bulawayo became a decision not to be taken lightly. Bulawayo represented a political minefield where Zanu-PF and its leadership always had to tread cautiously.

Indeed, in recent years the city, 'a place of killing', became the setting for clashes between rival factions in the ruling Zanu-PF party. It was no surprise therefore that on Saturday 4 November 2017, Grace Mugabe, minutes into her speech at a rally at White City Stadium in Bulawayo, was booed and heckled by sympathisers and supporters of then vice-president Emmerson Mnangagwa. White City Stadium, located in the township of Pelandaba, is a focus of political activity. Political parties worth their salt convene rallies at the stadium, which has lush green grounds and a modern track and field, renovated in 2014 for the African Union Youth Games. Churches also host all-night prayer vigils at the stadium. In 1988 Jamaican reggae artist Gregory Isaacs performed at White City. When he appeared for less than an hour, fans began to demonstrate and nine people were injured after clashes with police at the stadium.

The booing of Grace Mugabe by Mnangagwa's supporters was an unexpected showdown, but it was hardly a shocking development. For months, Mnangagwa had maintained a stony silence as Grace went on the rampage, publicly denouncing him during a series of rallies held across the country in an attempt to discredit his ambition to succeed her ninety-three-year-old husband as president. However, the rally invective was no random denunciation. Zanu-PF was due to meet for its annual party conference in a month's time. Among the items on the agenda was the issue of succession. A faction in Zanu-PF known as Generation 40, or in its shortened form as G40, was pushing to have Grace elevated to become vice-president, with a view to possibly taking over from Robert Mugabe one day.

The Bulawayo Presidential Youth Interface rally was the ruling party's ninth such gathering and was expertly used by Grace to dress down Mnangagwa. While the previous eight rallies had followed the same pattern of castigation, Mnangagwa had not taken the bait and had appeared unmoved by Grace's stinging rebukes. This may have been a well-calculated strategy on Mnangagwa's part, whose nickname, 'the Crocodile', conjures images of immense patience and a canny ability to know when to seize the moment.

In the public view, Grace, a political novice with only three years in active politics, seemed to be overreaching herself and stepping out of line. Indeed, Mnangagwa was by no means the only senior party member she was targeting, with no regard for the consequences of her actions. A morbid fascination accompanied her public addresses, no doubt because her intention was unclear, despite widespread speculation about her ultimate ambition. What was the source of her gall? Was it centred on her status as Mugabe's wife? These and other questions lingered. Grace would often drop hints about the fount and source of her power, reminding audiences that she was the First Lady and the 'wife of Mugabe, the president'.

As for Mnangagwa, who is among the most feared politicians in the country, his prolonged silence had the effect on some of questioning his political stock. Was he still 'the Crocodile', or had he recoiled from Grace's attacks and turned into a 'lizard', as his critics mocked?

Grace, the head of the Zanu-PF Women's League at the time, was also the poster girl of the G40 faction. The term G40 was first coined by Jonathan Moyo, the higher education minister, in 2011. A staunch ally of the Mugabes, Moyo claims to have first used the term in an academic sense, referring to the demographics of the country, whose majority consists of young people under the age of forty. Still, as the Zanu-PF succession war unfolded, the G40 tag stuck and took on a life of its own. It came to refer to the faction in the ruling party most sympathetic to Grace Mugabe. Its leading lights were Moyo; Saviour Kasukuwere, the local government minister; and Patrick Zhuwao, the youth development, indigenisation and empowerment minister.

The G40 faction's aim was to push for a transfer of power to younger leaders, regardless of the fact that they were political novices and lacked liberation war credentials. The G40's stance was a godsend for Grace as it meant that she did not need to pose as a doyenne of the liberation struggle in order to succeed her husband. Her bid was backed by the Zanu-PF Youth and Women's Leagues. 'Munhu wese kuna amai', which means 'Everyone must support our mother', and

'One centre of power' were the rallying slogans popularised and chanted by these two party wings in support of Grace.

Hand in glove, these two groups – the Youth and the Women's Leagues – provided the G40 faction with a fierce support base and set themselves up against the old guard of liberation war fighters. The war veterans, who had participated in the 1970s Bush War that led to Zimbabwe's independence from Britain, clashed often with the G40 faction. The veterans were wary of what they saw as the possibility of state capture by the youth, while the G40 faction slapped down the war veterans for being irrelevant players in modern-day Zimbabwe.

The G40 faction's chief sworn enemy was Emmerson Mnangagwa. A liberation war hero, he was the prime embodiment of the old guard and the last remaining real hurdle to the seizure of power by the G40 faction. But Mnangagwa was no pushover. He had an impeccable track record in the Bush War, in Zanu-PF and in government. He had been loyal to Mugabe for almost fifty-four years, enjoyed a close relationship with members of the military's top brass, and had been in government since independence and served in various portfolios. He had been state security minister, rural housing minister, Speaker of Parliament, defence minister and justice minister.

In December 2014, Mnangagwa's already towering political stature received yet another boost when Mugabe picked him to be his vice-president during the party's elective congress that month. His elevation was seen by a faction sympathetic to his rise in power, the Lacoste group, as tacit endorsement that Mnangagwa was the natural choice as president after Mugabe. The Lacoste faction is named after the French international fashion brand that uses a crocodile as its symbol and logo. 'The Crocodile', as we have seen, is Mnangagwa's nickname.

Bullish in its approach, the Lacoste faction was headstrong in its demand that no one in Zanu-PF had the experience to succeed Mugabe except for Mnangagwa. After all, who else had a similar track record of loyalty and such unquestionable liberation war credentials as Mnangagwa? And with that line of thought, the battle lines were drawn between the Lacoste and the G40 factions. The Lacoste group endorsed Mnangagwa as heir apparent, while the G40 faction insisted that there was no anointed successor. This back-and-forth contest between the two persisted for the next three years after Mnangagwa's appointment as vice-president.

However, the event that really triggered the seismic shift that would change Zimbabwe's political landscape took place in November 2017. It was the Presidential Youth Interface rally in Bulawayo that marked the turning point. It was a make-or-break event not only for Zanu-PF's two warring factions but for the entire country. Here, the Lacoste faction for the first time openly challenged Grace Mugabe, who until then had run roughshod over its leader, Mnangagwa. The rally also exposed tensions that had been simmering for months in Zanu-PF and provided the catalyst for the chain of events over the following twenty-one days that changed Zimbabwe's political landscape.

The Bulawayo rally was always going to be the place where there would be bloodletting. The rally had already been postponed twice, with the organisers, the Zanu-PF Youth League led by Kudzai Chipanga, claiming a shortage of funds as the reason for the delay. Initially, the rally was set for early October. But in fact there were behind-the-scenes tensions, as both the Zanu-PF Youth League and the G40 faction were wary of the groundswell of support that might emerge for Mnangagwa. Insiders who spoke off the record said the G40 faction was aware of the intention of the Lacoste faction to openly push back against Grace Mugabe in Bulawayo. By postponing the rally, the Zanu-PF Youth League sought to buy time, as it plotted a way to contain the plan by its rivals to turn out in numbers and show support for Mnangagwa.

To counter Lacoste, a scheme was hatched to reduce the number allowed entry into the stadium for the rally, with the intention of increasing the number of G40 members. Consequently, the organisers of the rally and members of the G40 faction printed a certain number of T-shirts that would be handed over only to members of the G40 faction to wear. These T-shirts would be used as a marker to identify supporters of the G40 faction, who would then be allowed entry into White City Stadium. Those without the T-shirts, presumably Lacoste faction sympathisers, would be denied entry and turned away.

Through its own networks, the Lacoste faction became aware of the counterplot by the G40 faction. They then duplicated the T-shirts distributed by the G40 faction and handed them over to their own members. In this way their supporters could pose as members of the G40 faction and be allowed entry into the stadium. About R50 000 was spent to buy the T-shirts from South Africa, according to an insider.

The insider elaborated on the strategy. 'On our side, we supported logistically the Zanu-PF youths that were pro-Mnangagwa. G40 had printed a certain number of T-shirts and made sure that only their people got them. So that when it comes to the gate, rather than showing your Zanu-PF card, by your T-shirt you were identified and could go in. We copied those same T-shirts. Magura Charumbira and his group had already met, the night before, and decided they were going to sing a specific song denouncing Grace. They had agreed that they were going to boo as soon as she started to say negative things.'

'On Friday, the eve of the rally, they practised songs', the insider added. 'There was this particular Ndebele song that they sang: "Into oyenzayo siyayizonda", which meant "What you are doing we hate it". It was do or die. They had insulted him [Mnangagwa] at every single rally. Bulawayo was seen as the last stand. Yes, there was still one more rally to go in Harare, but Bulawayo is where we thought we were going to stand up. Ironically, G40 thought that Bulawayo was where Mnangagwa would have no supporters. So when the booing started, Grace got agitated and the former president also got agitated. That's what triggered an emotional response from the former president. All those other times he had kept his cool and they would play good cop, bad cop; the wife would say something negative, he would say something mild and reconciliatory. But in this case, because she had been booed, he then showed his true colours, that he was up to something and actually wanted to get rid of his vice-president.'

Charumbira, the late Zanu-PF Bulawayo youth provincial chairperson, who died in a car accident in January 2018, was arrested after the rally. He was identified as the mastermind behind the booing and heckling of Grace.

Within forty-eight hours of the Bulawayo rally, Mugabe fired Mnangagwa from government. Tipped off about a plot against his life, Mnangagwa fled to Mozambique and eluded a manhunt launched by state security agents. In self-imposed exile in South Africa, Mnangagwa fought back against Mugabe and warned him that his own political career was not over. 'In a matter of weeks I will return to take over the party and government' was the promise that Mnangagwa made to Mugabe from exile.

A defiant Mugabe purged Mnangagwa's allies in Zanu-PF, right across the party's ten provinces. Senior party leaders such as Patrick Chinamasa, Kembo Mohadi and Oppah Muchinguri-Kashiri faced expulsion for their support of Mnangagwa.

Then, a week after Mnangagwa's dismissal, a military intervention was rolled out by the army commander, Constantino Chiwenga, who issued a warning to Mugabe to end the wide-scale party purges. The instability in the ruling party had become a threat to national security, he declared.

But Chiwenga's warning was ignored. Instead, a party spokesperson, Simon Khaya-Moyo, said the army chief's statements bordered on treason. Under Zimbabwean law, treason is punishable by death. Later in the day, army tanks were seen making their way into Harare's city centre.

In the early hours of Wednesday morning on 15 November 2017, the military announced to the nation on the state broadcaster that it had taken over the running of the country. 'Fellow Zimbabweans, the president and his family are safe and sound. We are just targeting the criminal elements around him,' announced Major-General Sibusiso Moyo.

Over the next few days, street protests were held by ordinary

Zimbabweans demanding an end to Mugabe's rule. Zanu-PF recalled the then ninety-three-year-old as party leader and also prepared to impeach Mugabe, issuing him with an ultimatum to resign. After a thirty-seven-year-long rule, Mugabe tendered his resignation on 21 November 2017, just as the impeachment process was under way in Parliament.

Within three days of Mugabe's resignation, Mnangagwa returned to the country after spending sixteen days in exile in South Africa and was inaugurated as the third president of Zimbabwe.

Behind the scenes, there were many people involved in assisting Mnangagwa's rise to power. These included political allies, family members, business associates, Zanu-PF party members and the military, who all played different roles in helping Mnangagwa stage a comeback that forced Mugabe's hand and led to the ultimate defeat of the G40 faction. All of them took risks of varying degree to help Mnangagwa. Many were unwilling to speak on the record for this book about their part in the events of November 2017 because of the sensitivity of their information.

What I gleaned through interviews with those willing to share their experiences is that while Mnangagwa's rise may have involved a calculated strategy, there was never any assurance of success. Mnangagwa, it seems in hindsight, also benefited from the blunders of his rivals. Grace Mugabe, the G40 faction and Robert Mugabe himself miscalculated in their joint push to remove him – mistakes that in the end proved fatal for them.

Power-hungry, Grace had made too many enemies during her short political career. As for the G40 faction, it smelt blood and celebrated its victory prematurely. In the process, it underestimated the Lacoste faction and attempted to ride roughshod over the war veterans and the army, the long-time kingmakers of Zimbabwe.

Robert Mugabe, for his part, misjudged the nature and extent of the succession fight that was under way in Zanu-PF. He was unable to realise that his long-time strategy of playing off rival factions in

Zanu-PF against each other had finally lost its effectiveness. Had he settled the burning question of a successor much sooner, perhaps the outcome of November would have been different and his legacy would have remained intact. Mugabe also misread the ferocity of his wife's political ambitions, his growing frailty, and the extent to which he had become isolated from his war-time colleagues, who were the key pillars of his rise and prolonged stay in power.

On 21 November 2017, Mugabe stepped off Zimbabwe's political stage after a denouement that lasted a matter of weeks. This was the ignominious end of a larger-than-life liberation hero, self-styled survivor and conqueror of white imperialism. During his final days in office, his fate was ultimately one of rejection. Rejection stared at him from his army, from ordinary citizens who staged street marches against him, and from the ruling party, Zanu-PF, over which he had presided for nearly four decades. There was no longer any other option but for him to take his leave.

2

The president's man

Larry Mavima is seated behind a large oak desk in his office, located in the upmarket suburb of Newlands in Harare, where I meet him. He wears a navy blue suit and a striped blue shirt. On his suit jacket, he has a prominent Zimbabwe flag pin. Mavima extends a firm handshake, smiles and apologises for not having made it to our appointment earlier in the morning. Spread out in front of him on his desk are some documents. He asks for a few minutes to get a few things out of the way, otherwise we will be continually disturbed by calls during the interview. I take a seat while he reaches for his phone, quickly responding to messages.

In the public's eye, Mavima has made a name for himself as an industrialist and businessman. It was, however, in politics where Mavima first cut his teeth and made his name. He was the Zanu-PF member of Parliament for the Zvishavane-Runde constituency from 2008 until 2013. He is also the former vice-chairperson of the Midlands province.

In March 2016, Mavima was appointed chairperson of the board of the NRZ, the railway parastatal headquartered in Bulawayo. At its peak in the 1990s, the NRZ employed about 12 000 workers. This number has since shrunk to just under 5 000, as the overall fortunes of the parastatal, since the turn of the millennium, have declined.

As the point man tasked by government to turn the NRZ around, Mavima is full of plans for the parastatal's revival. In February 2018, he signed off on a $400-million rail-rehabilitation scheme. The deal is expected to increase business and generate more revenues for the NRZ.

At the same time, Mavima's political roots remain intact and he is a member of the Zanu-PF Central Committee. This 300-member Soviet-style body has the responsibility of making decisions for the ruling party outside its annual conference. It is the same Zanu-PF Central Committee that recalled Mugabe in 2017 as leader, a few weeks before a party congress was set to be staged.

More significant, politically, is the close and personal relationship Mavima has with Emmerson Mnangagwa. Mavima has been by Mnangagwa's side for twenty-seven years, since 1991. A few days after Mnangagwa took the oath of office in 2017, *NewsDay* described Mavima as 'the brains behind Mnangagwa's ascendancy'. An ally and confidant of Mnangagwa, Mavima is the president's man.

The trust that Mnangagwa has in Mavima also stems from the fact that the two men come from the same rural area in Zvishavane. Mnangagwa has often spoken about his simplicity to audiences and stressed that he is a mere villager from Zvishavane. Mavima is from the Masunda area, while Mnangagwa is from the nearby Mapanzure area.

Given the high tensions that were a strong feature of the succession battle in Zanu-PF and the deep suspicions each faction harboured against the other, it is understandable why Mnangagwa counted on those who had almost become family to assist him.

Mavima is not only a personal friend of Mnangagwa. He is also looked up to by Mnangagwa's children, who affectionately call him 'Uncle Larry'. During Mnangagwa's self-imposed exile in South Africa, Mavima became the de facto spokesperson for Mnangagwa and his family. It was a role that carried great personal risk. In addition, it also clearly showed that Mavima was in contact with Mnangagwa, who was then wanted by the authorities in Zimbabwe.

'The threats that were coming through were coming from Jonathan Moyo,' says Mavima. 'He was motivating for me to get arrested for treason. This was after the first press statement had been published because they knew that I had delivered the press statement and that I was the one who actually paid for the adverts. So the story that I was hearing from my internal security sources was that I was the main subject of their daily briefings. When they were telling me, they would say, "Larry Mavima knows where he [Mnangagwa] is and is communicating with him and so he is harbouring a fugitive." But I didn't know that he was a fugitive, because there had been no crimes that he had been charged with before he left.'

Mavima was put under state surveillance and his phone was bugged. As a result he was forced to ditch his Samsung smartphone and use a small old phone, as a safety precaution, to communicate with Mnangagwa.

Aware that his schedule and affairs were known to the state security agents who were tailing him, Mavima also had to change his daily routines. He stopped going to his office, spent the night in different locations away from his home, and worked from different places. He also stopped driving his regular cars.

'But things really came to a boiling point when my connection in the Central Intelligence Organisation [CIO] and very close friend, who happened to have very strong ties with the G40 faction, actually came home and said, *Mkoma* [brother], I can't go to sleep without talking to you today. Things are not good out there for you. I think the best thing is for you to get out of the country for a while, because they are really after you,' he recalls.

There were telltale signs that some sort of physical harm could head his way. In his neighbourhood of Greendale, his house was the only one that would experience unexplained power cuts for long periods of time.

As a safety precaution, Mavima left Zimbabwe on Saturday 11 November 2017 and only returned a week later, on 18 November.

When he left the country, he was escorted through the airport in Harare by a friend in the intelligence services. He left by himself and headed first for Dubai and then proceeded to India. He later returned again to Dubai.

Although he was outside Zimbabwe, he continued to pursue his role of mobilising support for Mnangagwa. This included designing posters and T-shirts that would be used in street marches and demonstrations against Mugabe in the main cities of Harare and Bulawayo. 'We were designing the posters and saying yes to this one and no to this one. We would then send those to him [Mnangagwa] and he would make the decisions. There was one which said "Zuma voetsek" [Zuma, get lost] but Mnangagwa said, No, we can't have that one. I remember it all vividly.'

Exiled in South Africa at the time, Mnangagwa preferred to exercise caution than to clash with Jacob Zuma, then the South African president. Zuma, who was also the chairperson of the Southern African Development Community (SADC), had dispatched special envoys to Zimbabwe to form part of the discussions around the country's political transition. Zuma's efforts, however, angered ordinary Zimbabweans, who feared that the regional powerhouse would seek a return to the status quo under Mugabe and resist a transfer of power in Zimbabwe. There is also a long history of disappointment on the part of the main opposition party, the Movement for Democratic Change, with the regional bloc. The MDC claims that SADC has always taken Mugabe's side and treated him with kid gloves, even when he violated the principles of free and fair elections and human rights upheld by SADC.

But for his campaign of such a scale in support of Mnangagwa, in which large resources were needed, I ask Mavima what the size of his financial war chest was, and where the financing came from. With a shrug of his big shoulders, he is dismissive. 'There was no budget. We were just reaching out to sympathisers who were mostly Zimbabweans and it was not a lot of money that was spent. All in all, we must have spent about $30 000 to $40 000. The money was used on posters, T-shirts and newspaper adverts, because the second statement also had to be paid for. We were now using more than one newspaper and had *NewsDay*, *Daily News* and had also gone into *The Herald*.'

Although the two men were now temporarily based in different parts of the world, what is clear is the resolve and determination by those in Mnangagwa's inner circle to mount a challenge to Mugabe and ensure that Mnangagwa did not go quietly.

In exile in Dubai, Mavima also closely followed the announcement made by the military in the early hours of 15 November 2017 on the state broadcaster, the Zimbabwe Broadcasting Corporation (ZBC). As he puts it, Mavima said that announcement confirmed that the situation was now at a different level.

'When I saw Major-General S.B. Moyo on TV, I knew that this was the endgame. I had other connections within the army that I was talking to and they also had given me the assurance that, Look, this thing can only go one way; the man [Mugabe] has to go and he is going to go, it's just a question of time. Yes, they were negotiating, but the decision had been made that he had to go and it was now about trying to find the right way for him to go. So there was determination on their part to make sure that the transition had to happen and there was concern also among them that if it didn't work out, definitely they would be the first to go to the gallows.'

* * *

As one of the few privileged enough to have the president's ear, Mavima has insight into Mnangagwa's mind. Over the long years of his political career, Mnangagwa has often been cast as a politician to be feared. Mnangagwa's nickname 'Crocodile' forms part of this aura, which he has used in the battles with his political rivals.

However, during the tensions that escalated with Grace Mugabe at the Presidential Youth Interface rallies in 2017, it seemed that

Mnangagwa's political persona, built over many years, was rapidly losing purchase. The persistent question that began to emerge was whether Mnangagwa really was the all-powerful politician he had been made out to be. Opinions in the public arena were mixed. While his supporters were at pains to defend him, his opponents tore him down, questioning whether he really was a 'Crocodile' or just a mere 'Lizard'. Mavima, however, scoffs at this caricature of Mnangagwa and insists that it was precisely his ability to withstand the heat brought to bear on him by Grace Mugabe that showed the strength of his character. 'If it had been other people, they would have just walked away. It would have been the same as walking away from a fight, but Mnangagwa stood his ground,' he says.

Mavima leans forward and puts his right index finger on one of the papers in front of him, as if to emphasise his next point.

'This whole issue started way back. It was a concerted effort to humiliate and frustrate the then vice-president [Mnangagwa] into resigning. They thought that he would go the easy way, the way that the former vice-president Joice Mujuru went. When she got attacked, she just basically coiled into a cocoon and disappeared from the face of the earth and people did whatever they wanted. But this was not to be with this man. He said, "I am not going to run away from these guys. I am going to attend every Youth Interface rally that I can, together with my wife. I don't care what rubbish they throw at me. It's all designed to humiliate me." That's what he [Mnangagwa] used to tell us.'

On 2 June 2017, Zanu-PF launched the first of its Presidential Youth Interface rallies in Marondera, a town some seventy-six kilometres from the capital, Harare. The purpose of the rallies, organised by the Zanu-PF Youth League, was to give youths in the country an opportunity to meet President Mugabe and share their concerns with him. In turn, Mugabe would cleverly use the rallies as an election campaign platform and canvass for votes from the youths for the 2018 elections. Young people make up about 60 per cent of Zimbabwe's thirteen million population. The rallies gave Mugabe an edge over competitors, as he had clinched the endorsement of Zanu-PF, at the party's annual conference in December 2016, to stand as its presidential candidate in the 2018 elections.

The rallies of 2017 provided the strongest sign that Zanu-PF's election machine was on the move and in full swing. At the time, the country's main opposition parties were at a standstill, deeply divided over the composition of the alliance that would stand against Mugabe. Morgan Tsvangirai, then leader of the Movement for Democratic Change and long-time arch-rival of Mugabe, was faced with a challenge from Joice Mujuru to lead the opposition alliance. All these disagreements in the opposition's ranks worked in Zanu-PF's favour.

However, it did not take long before the rallies deviated from their main purpose. Soon they turned into a public show of the bitter rivalry in Zanu-PF between its two main factions, the Lacoste and G40. For the G40 faction, the rallies enabled it to strengthen its hand by using Grace Mugabe as its mouthpiece and battering ram. One by one, she publicly hammered some of the leading lights of the Lacoste faction, with Mnangagwa being the ultimate target.

Although caught on the back foot by the way in which the rallies had shifted from their initial purpose, the Lacoste faction took stock and prepared to put up a fight. Wild cheers and praises were often given to Mnangagwa each time that he made an entrance at campaign venues and took to the podium to greet the crowds. The message from the Lacoste faction was unmistakably clear: Mnangagwa was popular and also had his own base of supporters. It is this show of support for Mnangagwa, which at times eclipsed even that given to the Mugabes, that infuriated Grace and the G40 faction. They became even more determined to push for the removal of Mnangagwa.

'The final straw was the Bulawayo one; they [G40] were now going for the jugular vein,' says Mavima. 'It is not correct to say that people were bused for purposes of booing the First Lady. The people were just upset. This is not the first time. Even during the time that the former vice-president [Joice Mujuru] was hounded out of office, people walked out on the First Lady. She [Grace] was also visibly upset at that time, way back in 2014. Maybe we should give credit to the people of Bulawayo for having the courage to express their displeasure, because that is the only province really that clearly demonstrated its dissatisfaction with the manner in which the First Lady was conducting herself in public by physically demonstrating, whether it was by booing or walking away.'

The booing of Grace Mugabe in Bulawayo, Mavima says, excited him as he saw it as the 'beginning of Zimbabweans getting their voice back'.

'Afraid? That is not the correct word to use about how I felt at the time, but I was anxious. That is to say, which way are we going to go now as a country? Are we going to collapse now into civil unrest, and what will this lead to?'

In Bulawayo, Robert Mugabe, visibly angered by the booing and heckling of Grace, issued his most direct threat to Mnangagwa. He said he had the power to fire his deputy if he realised he'd made a mistake in appointing him as his second-in-command.

The die was now cast between Zanu-PF's two factions.

* * *

On Monday 6 November, at around 4 p.m., President Mugabe announced to the nation that he had fired Mnangagwa as vice-president.

Journalists gathered inside the Information Ministry offices at Munhumutapa Building, waiting for Simon Khaya-Moyo, then the information minister, to address a hurriedly arranged press conference. Khaya-Moyo, as the government's spokesperson, was to provide the official confirmation that Mugabe had indeed axed Mnangagwa. It was by that time, however, an open secret that Mugabe had already made good on his threat delivered in Bulawayo to fire Mnangagwa. Khaya-Moyo, accompanied by George Charamba, Mugabe's former spokesperson and the permanent secretary at the Information Ministry, made it clear from the outset that he would not take any questions.

The brief statement made by Khaya-Moyo said Mugabe had fired Mnangagwa with immediate effect, for 'disloyalty' and for 'failure to execute his duties'. And just as quickly as it had been arranged, the press briefing ended.

In retrospect, it appears that Mnangagwa's dismissal that day as Zimbabwe's vice-president not only ended his long career of nearly forty years in government but also crucially ushered in the endgame that would see Mugabe fall from power.

That day, many other things came to an end, such as the decades-old relationship between Mugabe and Mnangagwa and the farcical front presented by Zanu-PF of a united party. It was now clear beyond any doubt that the party was deeply and bitterly divided along factional lines. The pussyfooting by Grace over her hidden ambitions to succeed her husband also came to an end. It was now starkly clear that Grace had set her eyes on being appointed vice-president at Zanu-PF's forthcoming December congress.

However, what was less clear at the time was that the military's top brass – with whom Mnangagwa was known to enjoy a close relationship – had decided to call time on its relationship with Mugabe. Briefly, Mugabe, the ever-artful political survivor, seemed to have won the upper hand yet again. But his victory was short-lived.

Across town, as Khaya-Moyo announced to the media that Mnangagwa was fired, Mavima, who had received information earlier in the morning from his contacts in the intelligence services of the vice-president's imminent ousting, was meeting with Mnangagwa at his Helensvale home, in the upmarket suburb of Borrowdale in Harare.

I ask Mavima what the first reaction of those in the inner circle to Mnangagwa's dismissal was.

'We huddled together and said, Look, this is very unfortunate. What do we do now? We then said, No, we don't want our vice-president

[Mnangagwa] to go the same way that Mujuru went, quietly, and he must issue a press statement.'

Mavima and his colleagues (whom he asked not to be named) then began to draft a press statement to respond to the firing.

'I then called him and said, *Shefu* [boss], I would like to come and see you. He said, You can come, I am at home. I said, Can I come around at six or seven tonight? He said, No, come now. We found him at home, he was alone with his wife and children, and then he narrated the story of what had happened. Then we tried to encourage him and said, Don't worry, God has a plan and things will change.'

It was then that Mnangagwa told Mavima he had a press statement that he wanted to issue but would only do so at an 'appropriate time'. 'His press statement would show and tell the people of Zimbabwe what had happened. But then he went through what we had also written, read it, made his changes, and said he would add a few more things. Then he signed it and gave it back to me. But he said, You will only publish it when I am out of the country and I am safe.'

* * *

When Mnangagwa eventually managed to leave the country, Mavima released the statement to the media. It is reproduced here in full and indicates Mnangagwa's intention to fight back against Mugabe, despite having been fired and stripped of his vice-presidency.

My family was banished to Zambia when I was still in primary school for resisting the oppressive rule of the white minority regime in 1955. This action hardened my resolve for justice and black empowerment.

I joined the United National Independence Party (UNIP) led by Dr Kenneth Kaunda at a tender age and have been active in politics ever since. At 18 years of age I was recruited by the late Willie Musarurwa to join Zapu and sent for military training to

Tanzania and Egypt. A year later, in August 1963 to be precise, I broke away with some cadres to join the newly formed Zimbabwe African National Union. I was subsequently sent for advanced military training in China which I completed in May 1964. Some of my group members were Edson Shirihuru, Lawrence Svosve, John Shonhiwa and James Mudavanhu. We became known as the famous Crocodile Group.

Despite the hardships of the times, we operated in Zimbabwe (Rhodesia) travelling entirely by foot in order to avoid arrest. Some of my colleagues were betrayed by sell-outs, arrested and hanged. The same fate befell me in 1965. I was arrested, tortured and sentenced to death. The death sentence was subsequently commuted on a technicality to ten years' imprisonment, which I served in various prisons in Zimbabwe while at the same time I advanced my education through correspondence. After my release, I was deported back to Zambia where I completed my Law Degree. After my Law Degree, I voluntarily left Zambia to join the Liberation struggle in Mozambique in 1976 where I was assigned as the Special Assistant to the President, Cde R.C. Mugabe.

This role was reconfirmed at the Chimoio Congress in 1977. I have been very close to the President ever since. We have avoided life-threatening situations together. I even doubled up as his personal bodyguard. In return, the President has passed on to me life skills which have put me in good stead throughout my long period in government. Our relationship has over the years blossomed beyond that of master and servant but to father and son. My mouth has never uttered a single foul word against the President nor have I ever contemplated bringing him harm in any way. I therefore find it preposterous that any sane person can lyrically direct such accusations towards me. Of late, I have been vilified beyond measure. My service to the party and government of Zimbabwe and my public and private posture towards my boss are well known. No amount of lies and convoluted thinking can diminish my loyalty to my party and the President. I have never appointed or surrogated myself in any position in the Party or in Government. I remain firm and resolute against those who plunder public funds and are used by foreign countries to destabilize the Party. These same people are brazenly protected in public by the First Lady, thereby making a mockery of our public institutions. I stand prepared, once again, to pay the ultimate price in defence of Zimbabwe.

I am not afraid of anyone or worried about my political future under the current 'Party Capture' that is being tolerated and condoned by the First Family. I implore all genuine members of Zanu-PF to reject this 'Party Capture' by a few individuals as I hereby do unequivocally. This is not the Zanu-PF we established with the late Dr J.M. Nkomo and other luminaries who have passed on. This is now a party controlled by undisciplined, egotistical and self-serving minnows who derive their power not from the people and party but from only two individuals in the form of the First Family, who have now privatized and commercialized our beloved institution. It is regrettable that after 37 years of unbroken service in government, I am now being hounded out by minnows who have no liberation credentials or clear understanding of our constitution in Zanu-PF. We must reject this insane and 'idiotic' habit of expelling and suspending members of the party merely because we differ in opinion or have brighter and more progressive ideas of improving the lives of our people, to quote Cde R.C. Mugabe's own adjective.

Your Excellency and First Secretary of Zanu-PF, it is sad and deplorable that you have allowed our Party to be hijacked by novices and external forces as well as individuals who have a proven record of treachery. This Party is NOT PERSONAL PROPERTY for you and your wife to do as you please. Now that you have clearly told the world that I am your enemy who has taken in excess of 50 years to formulate a plan to dispose of you, I now urge all the genuine members of the Party to determine for themselves who between the three of us, including your wife and the notorious G40 boys, is the enemy of the Party and who the real culprit is in destroying our beloved Zanu-PF. Zanu-PF is anchored on core values which promoted unity, peace and development regardless of ethnicity. I find it abhorrent and repulsive to separate the nation by region and province, which is anathema to our founding principles.

My emphasis is for the nation to unite to create peace and development. This particular accusation is nauseating when the First Lady prefers to have the song 'Zezuru Unconquerable' played and sung at rallies she has held many times over. Who is the tribalist here? I have been accused of committing treasonous acts dating back from 1980. This is not only fake but laughable and the President knows that. Why, why, the people are asking, did you keep this man for so long and not tried him for treason all these years? Those who violate our Party code of conduct because they think they have now outgrown Zanu-PF, are free to go and form their own parties. I will go nowhere. I will fight tooth and nail against those making a mockery against Zanu-PF's founding principles, ethos and values. You and your cohorts will instead leave Zanu-PF by the will of the people and this we will do in the coming few weeks as Zimbabweans in general now require new and progressive leadership that is not resident in the past and refuses to accept change. My conscience obliges me to uphold the code of conduct of my beloved party and I refuse to be drawn into a public circus. Religious gatherings should be used to preach love, peace and harmony, not to spread hate speech and political intolerance. It was regrettable that men and women of the cloth were abused this past Sunday (5 November 2017) by none other than the First Lady, who spewed fake news, unfair and irresponsible comments about myself and character in an atmosphere which should have focused on Peace, Love, Unity and Development. This is grossly unfair and I was never given a chance to defend myself or at least proffer an explanation for the false and malicious accusations made against me.

Fellow Zimbabweans, and specifically members of Zanu-PF, the time is now to say NO to Demi-Gods and people that are self-centered and only think of themselves and their families. Let us bury our differences and rebuild a new and prosperous Zimbabwe, a country that is tolerant of divergent views, a country that respects opinions of others, a country that does not isolate itself from the rest of the world because of one stubborn individual who believes he is entitled to rule this country until death. We want a country that gives every citizen the opportunity to prosper, to take care of their families, a country that encourages Zimbabweans to invest in their economy and contribute to the development of infra-structure for future generations. This is part of my vision for a rejuvenated Zimbabwe and particularly Zanu-PF, and as I leave this post for now, I encourage all loyal members of the party to remain in the party to register to vote as we will very soon control the levers of power in our beautiful Party and country. 'Let not your hearts be troubled, for peace, love, unity, development and prosperity are around the corner.' I will be communicating with you soon and shall return to Zimbabwe to lead you.

PAMBERI NE ZANU-PF!!!! PAMBERI NE ORIGINAL ZANU-PF!!! PASI NE G40

I would like my fellow citizens to know that I am now out of the country, and safe. My sudden departure was caused by incessant threats on my person, life and family by those who have attempted before through various forms of elimination including poisoning.

Cde E.D. Mnangagwa

3

A great escape

Collins Mnangagwa is smartly dressed in black trousers and a purple silk shirt. He wears two gold rings, one on his small finger on the right hand and a gold wedding ring on the left hand. A gold chain around his neck is also visible and dangles in his slightly unbuttoned shirt. Visibly striking in his office in Chisipite in Harare are the many portraits of him and his father. One, however, is markedly distinct.

'That large one is when he came for my graduation in China. That is Frederick Shava, now Zimbabwe's ambassador to the United Nations in New York,' he says, beaming. In the picture, Collins is in his graduation gown and is flanked on either side by his father and Shava. It is clear that he has a very close relationship with his father and his face lights up when he speaks of him. Fluent in Mandarin, Collins studied in China for seven years and holds an electrical engineering degree.

My curiosity as to why there was a Chinese woman and, later, a Chinese man at the reception area when I arrived is now satisfied. Collins explains that as he is fluent in Mandarin, some of his clients are Chinese and he does consultancy work for Chinese investors keen to invest in Zimbabwe. Later when I leave the office after our meeting, I count three Chinese men and a woman in the reception area who are also waiting to see him.

On the day that his father was fired, Collins recalls that between 9 a.m. and 9.30 a.m. there were already strong rumours doing the rounds on the social media platform WhatsApp that Mugabe had dismissed his vice-president. Collins received numerous phone calls from family members seeking confirmation, following the threats issued at the rally at the weekend in Bulawayo. Keen to get clarity, Collins called his father to find out.

'Ndadzingwa [I have been fired],' was the curt response his father gave him. As Collins was on his way to the office at the time, he immediately did a U-turn and drove to Helensvale, to his father's home. When he arrived, he found his father was unhappy that he'd come.

'What for? Why are you coming here?' Mnangagwa snapped.

'I could tell that he was already in a mood,' Collins says.

In the lounge at home, Collins found his father seated with Auxillia, his mother, and an uncle, his mother's brother. The mood in the house was sombre. His uncle was on the phone in an attempt to mediate with persons close to Mugabe to persuade him to rethink his decision. At the same time his mother was also making phone calls to Grace Mugabe. She wanted to find out if it was true that her husband had been fired and why the fallout between them had happened. Grace did not pick up her calls, however. The family was only much later informed by persons in the know that Grace had been in meetings with Ignatius Chombo, the finance minister, and Saviour Kasukuwere, the local government minister, and could not take her call.

But why is it that she was keen to speak to Grace, I ask.

'They wanted to find out what was going on and also so that they could meet. Dad, you could tell from the way he was seated that he was really upset and had closed himself up. I think Mum saw that and she wanted to find a way, because these guys have known each other for a very long time. It was so that they could sit down and talk about what was really going on. I think they wanted to ask if it really had to go that far. But she [Grace] was not answering.'

Unable to get a hold of Grace, his mother decided that her husband must just report for work as usual. Without any official confirmation as yet, it seems she had a sliver of hope that there might be no truth to the rumours that her husband had been fired.

Collins says that his father agreed with her and went to the car and headed for his office. As he was about to leave, he asked his son to get him a burger, as he had not yet eaten. He was told to take it to the office where he would soon be.

When Collins arrived at the Munhumutapa offices with his father's takeaway, he reported to the security clearance desk. There, he informed the security person that he had come to see his father. The response he was given clearly indicated that something was wrong; he was told that there was no one by the name of Mnangagwa who worked at the building.

'I quickly picked up the phone and I called Dad. I said to him, I am at the office and I have your food. Where are you? He said to me, Leave, leave there now and just come home.'

Somewhere along the way, as he left home for the office, Collins thinks that his father got solid confirmation from his sources that he had been fired by Mugabe. But he forgot to inform his son that he had decided to head back home.

At about midday, family members and friends began to arrive at Mnangagwa's house, as news spread among his inner circle that he had been dismissed. The official confirmation to the nation was to be delivered only at around 4 p.m. by Simon Khaya-Moyo, the information minister at the time. Among those who came to his home were lawyers Gerald Mlotshwa and Edwin Manikai. In a private conversation in his study, Mnangagwa asked them both, 'Right what shall we do?'

At 5.30 p.m. Mnangagwa received a phone call at home, which he took in his bedroom. When he came out, he appeared with a briefcase and went straight to Collins and his twin brother, Sean.

'Let's go. I need to leave here, they are coming to arrest me,' he told his sons.

Without saying goodbye to the people in the house, Collins, his brother and their father slipped out of the house undetected. Collins drove off to Crowhill with Mnangagwa seated in the back of the vehicle. The property in Crowhill belongs to Collins and houses a partially complete building that is still under construction. Collins's reason for taking his father there was that those who were looking for him were unlikely to think of searching for him at a half-built and uninhabited property.

Once there, the brothers sat down next to their father, who explained to them what was happening. He had not spoken to them since they had left home.

'What they want to do is to catch me. Once they have caught me, they are going to put me in jail and then they are going to inject me. In the morning, everyone will be told that I hung myself,' the father explained to his sons.

It is significant that although Mnangagwa had been axed at the time, he was still being forewarned by insiders in the intelligence system of the plans being stitched together by the establishment. It revealed two important things about the prevailing situation. Firstly, it laid bare the extent to which Mnangagwa had eyes and ears deep within the security structures of government. These insiders were so loyal to him that they were able to provide him with authentic and trustworthy tip-offs about the plans of his enemies. The tip-offs that he received also revealed the extent of the political divisions in Zanu-PF, which had in turn permeated Zimbabwe's security forces. The factions within the security structures were deeply suspicious of each other, being divided in their loyalties to the president and to his vice-president. This later became even more evident in the attempt by the police and members of the Central Intelligence Organisation to arrest Mnangagwa at the border. Mnangagwa's eventual exit from the country was in fact facilitated by the military, which had fallen under his watch when he was defence minister from 2009 until 2013.

Past experiences convinced Mnangagwa not to downplay the tip-offs that he had received. If he failed to act on the information, he would be at the mercy of his political rivals should they carry out their plan to arrest him. He had already had a close shave with death in August

2017 after being poisoned during a Youth Interface rally in Gwanda, a town south-east of Bulawayo.

Upon hearing of the assassination plot, the two brothers reassured their father that they would stay by his side and would not allow him to be harmed. Their elder brother, Emmerson Jnr, then joined them. He was accompanied by another person whose name cannot be disclosed, by their brother Kuda David Mnangagwa, and a cousin-brother, Tarirai David Mnangagwa. There at the half-built house, the small group of seven hatched a scheme to take their father out of the country. Emmerson Jnr suggested that medical reasons be used as a decoy for his exit. The explanation that would be put forward as a reason for his emergency evacuation was that the events of the day had left their father shocked and overwhelmed and had resulted in him collapsing; he needed to go to South Africa to see a doctor urgently.

'But then complications started to come up; he needed a Zimbabwean doctor to first come and check him, an ambulance had to come and fetch him, and clearances were also needed at the airport. There were just a lot of things that were needed for that to happen. Time was ticking by,' says Collins.

All the same, a doctor's letter was later written by Air Commodore Dr Jasper Chimedza, who referred Mnangagwa to a South African doctor for urgent medical attention. Chimedza indicated in his letter that his patient was suffering from oesophagitis and gastritis. The referral letter, dated 6 November 2017, was addressed to a Dr Motora of Milpark clinic in Johannesburg and read: 'As you recall, he was previously there with similar problems. The current condition has been triggered by stress. Kindly assist and advise.'

But unfortunately for Mnangagwa, this attempt came to a dead end. In spite of the referral letter from a local doctor, there was no medical air rescue plane available to airlift Mnangagwa immediately to South Africa. The family was advised that a plane would only arrive the following morning from South Africa.

Should they find an alternative route or wait a little longer for the air rescue plane to arrive? That was now the nerve-racking decision faced by the family members.

Desperate and running out of options, they made frantic calls for help to friends and associates of Mnangagwa. Those approached were mostly either noncommittal or, in some cases, openly unwilling to assist the beleaguered former vice-president. Suddenly, association with Mnangagwa had become very risky and any persons thought to be aligned to him, or seen to even attempt to assist him, were likely to put themselves in harm's way and invite the full wrath of the authorities.

Collins remembers that time of rejection when they desperately asked friends and associates for help for their father's sake and singled out a mining company with interests in the Midlands area. 'African Chrome Fields said their airplane was broken down. Can you imagine?' he says.

This refusal by African Chrome Fields was confirmed by another person interviewed. 'They said, No, we don't want to [help]; we are here just to do mining. They refused even though they had a plane parked there at the Robert Gabriel Mugabe International Airport.'

Having drawn no luck with the aeroplane, the suggestion was made that he should travel by road and leave the country through the Forbes border post. The majority, however, favoured waiting it out in the hope of securing an aeroplane, which was seen as less risky and involving a shorter travel time.

'We were arguing amongst ourselves: some were pro the airplane route, some were pro the border route. But the guys who wanted the border route in the end were successful. It was around about 9 p.m. or 10 p.m. and we finally decided to go with the aeroplane route. So we went back home to Helensvale and there were just one or two relatives milling around.'

In the company of his sons, Mnangagwa returned to his house in preparation for leaving again once an aeroplane had been secured. Two men known by Collins as Limpin Jack and Geezer – actually, Hosea Manzunzu and Wise Jasi – also arrived. They went to speak to his father for about ten minutes. Afterwards, Mnangagwa informed his sons, 'We are now going to go by road.' None of them argued with him and they all offered to accompany him. His wife quickly packed a small bag for him in preparation for the trip.

Collins remembers that by that time all the official security assigned him at the house had been removed. While vice-president, he had been accustomed to living under protection provided by the state and there had even been a tent for soldiers in the grounds of his home. Now, he and his family had been left vulnerable and, except for the few relatives milling about, there was no one else to stay behind with Mnangagwa's wife.

'The gate was wide open. Everything had been removed, even the two cooks were withdrawn,' says Collins.

With the decision as to how to leave the country finally made, the group left for Mutare. 'When we left Helensvale it was about midnight and we travelled in three cars. Dad was in one of the cars with those two men who had come to see him, Limpin Jack and Geezer. I had my car and Emmerson Jnr's PA had another car. We drove, and luckily there were no roadblocks along the way. At about 3.30 a.m. or 4.00 a.m. we reached an inn. It's the inn along Christmas Pass just before you get to Mutare. That's where we went. Dad said, Let's rest there because the border anyway opens at six in the morning.'

Tired, the group prepared to put up for the few remaining hours before daybreak. Collins remembers that his father did not sleep; he just sat up with his brown Louis Vuitton briefcase by his side until dawn. At about 5.45 a.m., Mnangagwa woke the group up. It was time to leave for Forbes border post between Zimbabwe and Mozambique.

* * *

The first vehicles to arrive at the gate at Forbes were the small convoy of three cars in which Mnangagwa was travelling. The border post was already abuzz with dealers and traders who buy second-hand clothes from Mozambique for resale in Zimbabwe. They provided the perfect cover that the group needed in order to avoid detection by the authorities.

It was Hosea Manzunzu, or Limpin Jack as he is called, who took everyone's passports to be stamped and went inside the immigration hall. The entourage accompanying the former vice-president comprised eight people: their father, Emmerson Jnr, Sean, Collins, Jennifer, Tarirai, Wise Jasi, Manzunzu and Richard Mavoro. Mavoro was the head of security at the private company that guarded Mnangagwa's house. After Mavoro heard that Mnangagwa had been fired, he went to his house to offer his support and sympathy to the family. When Mnangagwa and the sons prepared to leave for the border, he immediately asked if he could be part of the group in order to help provide Mnangagwa with a safe passage.

Once the stamped passports were returned, Mnangagwa, who had not alighted from the car, gave an instruction that Collins, Sean and Mavoro must head back to Harare to look after his wife. Mnangagwa would only cross over into Mozambique with Emmerson Jnr, Manzunzu and Tarirai.

Manzunzu drove to the boom gate for the final security checks before proceeding into Mozambique, with Mnangagwa seated at the back. The vehicle was stopped at the gate by security and, instead of allowing it to pass through, the security personnel began to ask questions. Who were the people in the car? What was in the vehicle? They also demanded to search the vehicle.

'It started off with just three guys, but after ten minutes it was about seven. At that point it was Dad and Limpin Jack inside the car. Everyone else who was with him, Emmerson Jnr, Tarirai and Manzunzu, were outside the car and were talking to the guards. It was only later that we learnt that they were buying time as they waited for backup. We were told that seven heavily armed police in Ford Rangers arrived at the border post when we had already left. Some of the actions we took that day, I always say that it was God.'

Collins's car, a white Mercedes-Benz, was still parked outside the border post. The decision to leave it there later turned out to be a blessing in disguise, as we shall see. Because his father had said he and the others must return back to Harare and look after their mother, Collins was seated in his car waiting for confirmation from his brother Emmerson Jnr that they had managed to cross the border. But confirmation was not forthcoming. Collins became anxious and finally decided to call his brother to find out if they had made it. He then heard that they were stuck at the boom.

'I walked back to the boom gate. It's a bit of a distance from where the car was. When I got there, there were now about fifteen people surrounding the car. Tarirai was arguing with about six or seven of them and there were more people looking at their passports in their little office. I then went to Sean to find out what was happening, and all he could say was, It's tight, bro.'

Collins told Sean to tell his father that they needed to leave. It was clear that the situation had become desperate. In an effort to bring calm to the situation, they even offered the police and intelligence officers some money to allow the vehicle to cross over into Mozambique. This was refused.

Realising that no headway was being made, Mnangagwa finally sneaked out from the back of the vehicle. Wearing a cowboy hat and sunglasses, he walked back to Collins's car, which was parked outside the border post. When Collins saw his father alight from the vehicle, he immediately ran to his Mercedes. Now inside, Collins watched his father through the rearview mirror walk towards him. The first fifty metres that Mnangagwa took after slipping out of his vehicle went unnoticed: the security personnel at the gate were still caught up in heated exchanges with family members. Mnangagwa also received some cover from the hive of activity at the border post. There were lots of people about and a long queue of buses and trucks had formed as well.

'But in a split second, the CIOs [Central Intelligence Organisation operatives] realised that Dad had got out of the car. You could just see jackets flying and they ran after him to try and catch him, but he just kept on walking. Some CIOs who did manage to reach him were afraid to lay their hands on him. Some words were exchanged. In a flash, fists started to fly. Sean and Mavoro, who had also run after Dad, were punching some of the CIOs and they fell down. When one of the guys with the CIOs saw that Dad was not stopping and that a fight had broken out, he ran off and told the cops by the gate to go and get an AK-47 inside the police tent. "Tora AK! Tora AK!" [Get an AK! Get an AK!]'

The policeman thus instructed came out with an AK-47 assault rifle.

'When Dad saw that an AK-47 had been collected, he ran, but it wasn't that much of a distance. Sean was fighting with another guy, so he was now alone. One of the cops who had remained by the gate attempted to try and grab Dad. Then I got out and he just stopped what he was trying to do. Dad got into the car at the front next to me and somehow Mavoro managed to jump into the backseat and sat behind Dad. I could see Sean in my rearview mirror running towards the car. Because my window was open, the policeman with the AK-47 pointed it down at my head. But fortunately Sean ran to him and lifted up the barrel of the gun and tripped the policeman, who fell down to the ground.'

Gripped by panic and fear, Collins struggled to drive off. The gears would not engage as his door was slightly open. His father, sitting next to him, looked at him wondering why he was not driving off. 'When I realised why I couldn't engage the gear, I shut my door, put it into gear and drove off at high speed,' Collins says. 'The delay had been only a few seconds, but at that time it felt like ages. The police couldn't even get the number plate. That was just how quickly I raced off and how much dust I raised when I drove away from the border post.'

* * *

An internal security memorandum provides the official version by police of the events that took place at the Forbes border post. According to this confidential police security report, at about 5.30 p.m. on 6 November 2017, Detective Assistant Inspector Chivasa of the Criminal Investigation Department in Mutare was on duty with his team deployed at Forbes border post when Hosea Manzunzu, an ally of Mnangagwa, arrived from Harare. Manzunzu was driving a silver Mercedes-Benz ML350. Manzunzu said he wanted to clear the vehicle for temporary export to Beira in Mozambique, where he was conducting shipping business. Before the clearance of the vehicle could be completed, Manzunzu informed the detectives that he had decided to cancel his journey as he had received an urgent call from Harare and had been instructed to return. Manzunzu was the only occupant of the vehicle.

The following day at about 5.30 a.m. Chivasa received an instruction from his superiors from Mutare to be on high alert and monitor the movements of high-profile politicians at Forbes border post. If he noticed any such persons, he must alert the command station for further instructions. At about the same time, Manzunzu returned to Forbes with the same vehicle in which he wanted to cross into Mozambique.

Unlike the previous day, when he had been by himself, Manzunzu now had passengers. During the verification of those accompanying him, it was discovered that they included former vice-president Mnangagwa and his sons, as well as Tarirai Mnangagwa and Wise Jasi. There were also four middle-aged unidentified male adults who were Mnangagwa's bodyguards and whose two vehicles were parked outside the border post.

Further details from the official security report indicate that Chivasa communicated with Mutare as he sought instructions on how to handle the entourage.

'As the detectives were waiting for instructions from command, the former vice-president sneaked out of the Mercedes-Benz ML350 with two of the unidentified bodyguards and walked towards the exit gate back into Zimbabwe. The registration plates of the vehicle could not be mastered because of the skirmishes,' the security report read. Since the detectives were still waiting for instructions from command, efforts were made to stop the former vice-president from leaving the border. These were met with stiff resistance by the former vice-president and his bodyguards, who threatened detectives with assault if any further attempts were made to stop them.

Chivasa ordered Constable Dube of the Zimbabwe Republic Police's Support Unit, who was deployed at Forbes border post, to fire warning shots to stop the former vice-president and his party from fleeing, before the issue could be finalised. Dube, however, failed to issue a warning shot as one of the bodyguards grabbed the firearm. The distraction enabled Mnangagwa to get into another Mercedes-Benz, white in colour, which was parked about five metres from the gate, and it drove off at high speed to Mutare. The detectives went back to the exit gate where Manzunzu and his party were awaiting clearance. Instructions were later received from CID Mutare to release the vehicle and its occupants. Manzunzu and Jasi proceeded to Mozambique, while Tarirai Mnangagwa cancelled the journey, alleging that all his business documents were with his father. 'Tarirai Mnangagwa was interviewed and stated that he is the personal family aide to Emmerson Mnangagwa. After the official announcement of immediate relief of his duties as vice-president of Zimbabwe, he was assigned to protect and escort him to Beira in Mozambique for a period not spelled out due to the current prevailing situation.'

4

Jumping the border

After their narrow escape from Forbes border post, Mnangagwa, Collins and Mavoro did not go to Mutare town. Instead, Mnangagwa directed his son to a property hidden somewhere in the bush, so that they could avoid detection by the authorities. The reason was that state security agents would likely be on high alert at the border town, on the lookout for him. For his own safety, he had to remain undetected.

The episode at the border post appears to have shaken Mnangagwa. So troubled was his father that Collins remembers that for the first time he heard him speaking to himself – something that was unusual.

At about 7 a.m. they arrived at the property deep within the bush, which would be their temporary hideout before they moved on again. A bit more composed by now, his father joked that his son should get rid of his white Mercedes-Benz.

'Dad said to me, Your car won't do: you need to dispose of it. I said, I can't do that. So he said, All right, let's cover it. So we started pulling off branches from trees to throw over it.'

At their new hideout, whose owner Collins later became aware of but asked not to be named, there was a little cottage as well as a main house. The owner of the property allowed Mnangagwa to use only the cottage. Because of the skirmishes at the border post, their entourage had been separated. At that time, no one knew the whereabouts of the others. Some of Mnangagwa's mobile phones and his brown brief-case had also been left inside the vehicle that was prevented from passing through the boom gate into Mozambique.

'Dad asked if I knew where his briefcase was and I said, I don't know where it is. He then said, Go back and get it. I was shocked and I said, You want me to go back there where we just came from? Under no circumstances am I going to go back to that border post.'

Unbeknown to the trio, by some stroke of luck Collins's siblings had managed to leave the Forbes border post and make their way into Mutare's CBD. His brother Sean called Collins on his mobile phone and explained that he had tripped up the policeman with the AK-47, kicking the rifle away, and that the policeman had suffered an epileptic attack. While he was disarmed and on the ground, Sean had used the opportunity to escape.

The policeman who had tried to apprehend Mnangagwa had closed the gate of the border post, thus preventing the exit and entry of vehicles. This meant that the entourage's two vehicles were stuck within the border. While the border post was temporarily closed, Emmerson Jnr took his father's briefcase out of the vehicle that had been stopped from leaving and hid it in the second vehicle, which he locked. Making use of the commotion and panic that had erupted among the traders and vendors, who were alarmed by what had happened, Emmerson Jnr and his PA walked through a pedestrian gate and left. His cousin-brother Tarirai and Manzunzu were, however, not so fortunate. They were detained by the police and security officers at the border post.

On their way to Mutare by taxi from the border post, Emmerson Jnr saw his young brother Sean on the run in the veld. The taxi driver stopped and picked him up – and that was how the two brothers were reunited, although they were then not sure of the whereabouts of their father and Collins.

In a bid to reassemble everyone once again, Collins went and waited along the main road for Sean, who used a taxi to come and pick him up. Collins left his father under the care of Mavoro, who sat outside the cottage and guarded the former vice-president.

While Sean fetched Collins, Emmerson Jnr went to see some Zanu-PF friends of his in Mutare to ask for help in assisting their father to leave the country. Together once again, Collins and Sean set out for Mutare town, where they bought food – chicken and chips – and some water to take back to their father and Mavoro.

When the three brothers finally met up in Mutare, they spoke with some Zanu-PF officials who promised to help them take Mnangagwa out of the country. As a sign of their commitment to help, the party members gave the sons two old cars to use in order to avoid detection.

Unbeknown to the brothers, while they were still in town, the police were conducting searches in hotels and lodges and making door-to-door visits to houses that they suspected could offer refuge to Mnangagwa. On the way back to the cottage where their father was hiding out, Collins saw a vehicle drive past them flashing its lights. It later turned out that it was carrying his father and Mavoro. They had been removed from their hideout by the owner of the property and had been driven off somewhere else while the property was being searched by the police.

'That car later came back. Mavoro had recognised me in my T-shirt as I sat in the front. They had left that place because they had got information from the guy who stayed there that the police were now going door to door where they thought we could be. It was danger-ous; we didn't have anywhere to go. So Dad came back, with Mavoro and the driver. He was really looking drained and you could see that he was tired. This is someone who from yesterday when he was fired hadn't yet slept. The people that we had come with from Zanu-PF, when they saw him, they started crying. That was their first reaction and that's just how bad he was looking. They were asking themselves if that's how bad things had come to.'

Afraid of the danger to which he would expose the Zanu-PF members who had offered to assist, Mnangagwa pleaded with them to simply put him in the boot of their car while taking him out of the country and not attempt anything that could bring harm their way.

By then, news of the fracas at the border post had reached Harare. Mnangagwa's wife called her husband and sons, urging them to return home and use legal ways to fight whatever charges might be trumped up against her husband. Auxillia insisted that the family would be able to find lawyers that could defend her husband against any accusations brought by Mugabe's regime. But Mnangagwa was equally emphatic. He would not go back to Harare.

Holed up in the bush, and on the run, the group needed to devise a second plan for leaving the country. It then became apparent that Manzunzu and Jasi's scheme to go by road and cross via Forbes border post had not been well thought out: the entourage had come face to face with a determined bid to stop them, and a family member, Tarirai, had been detained.

Avoiding Mnangagwa's capture was the immediate concern of the group, given the failure to cross legally at the border post that morning. Collins recalls that they asked his father to change his clothes in order to avoid detection. 'Dad was wearing a white shirt. We said, No, you will be caught in that bright shirt. So he had to put on a really tight grey shirt that belonged to Sean. It was bad. But what else could we do?'

Desperate for help, Mnangagwa called another friend in Mutare who offered to put him up. Accompanied by Sean and Mavoro, he left and made his way to where he would be given temporary shelter. But before he did so, Collins remembers his father's last instructions. These were crystal clear: before nightfall, Emmerson Jnr had to find a crossing point that they could use to enter Mozambique.

* * *

Running out of time, and with night approaching, Emmerson Jnr and Collins held further secret meetings with Zanu-PF party officials and military personnel.

'Sean and Mavoro then came to us after they had dropped Dad off. They left him with only one phone to communicate with us when we were ready to move. We had a team that dedicated itself to help him and they said they would rather die in the bush with their leader than allow the rubbish that was happening, and these guys were from military intelligence. The initial plan that they came up with was that we were going to cross at the same point. They said, We are military and no one searches our cars. Their reasoning was that no one expects you to cross using the same route.'

The initial plan was to cross over into Mozambique at 7 p.m. But before then, three reconnaissance trips were carried out in which the military personnel crossed over into Mozambique to reconnoitre the situation on the ground. After the final trip they called to inform the brothers of the immense difficulties that faced them. Roadblocks had been mounted by police and they were not asking for driver's licences, but instead they wanted drivers to switch on the lights inside their cars and to open their car boots as well.

During the reconnaissance trips to assess the situation, the brothers took the opportunity to enlist the help of the men from military intelligence to collect Mnangagwa's brown briefcase from the car left behind at the border post. Collins says the police tried to prevent the military personnel from getting access to the vehicle, but the police and the intelligence operatives were beaten up. When Mnangagwa was finally handed his briefcase, he was delighted to get it back. He still uses it today.

As their initial scheme of crossing at the border post was no longer viable, a new plan was developed by which they would enter Mozambique at Marymount, an illegal crossing point. The initial team put together to assist in the operation was reduced. Instead of the fifteen or so who had been involved, the number was whittled down to just three. Suspicions and doubts appear to have begun to creep in.

Mnangagwa was informed of the new plan and so was ready when he was called. At about 7 p.m., the extraction team began its reconnaissance trip at Marymount and provided regular updates to Emmerson

Jnr and Collins. Then at about 10.30 p.m., Collins received a call from African Chrome Fields, the mining company that has interests in the Midlands province in Zimbabwe. 'Chinaman – they call me Chinaman because I studied in China – I am trying to get hold of your brother [Emmerson Jnr], his phones are off. I don't know where he is. In the next five minutes you are going to get a call from the minister of defence, Sydney Sekeramayi. He has spoken to the powers that be and they want him to come back. In fact they want him to attend tomorrow's Politburo. Tell him they want to reassure him that nothing will happen to him. Please, please, please make sure he talks to Sekeramayi.'

Collins informed his brother Emmerson Jnr of the call and sought advice on what to do. Emmerson Jnr instructed Collins not to inform them or anyone else that they were together or that they had any contact with their father. 'Tell them you are in Shurugwi, at the mine, and we are not together,' Emmerson Jnr told his young brother.

Five minutes later, a call came through from Simukai Sekeramai, the son of the defence minister. Collins put the call on speakerphone so that his brother could also listen in.

'You could tell that the call was on speakerphone on his side. It's 10.30 p.m., it's late, what's up?' Collins said.

'I have an understanding that you are with your father,' Simukai said.

'I am actually not with him, I am at the mine,' Collins replied.

'Do you know where he is?' Simukai persisted.

'Then I overheard Sekeramayi talking to his son and saying, Tell him to speak the truth. We have a message for his father from Number One that we need to give him,' Collins said.

'Collins, look, you don't need to be afraid, I want to reassure you that everything is fine, nothing is going to happen to your Dad. You need to pass on a very important message to your Dad from H.E. [His Excellency]. He doesn't need to run,' Simukai said.

'Look, as soon as I get word from him or see him, I will tell him,' Collins replied before hanging up.

Why was it so important for Sekeramayi, the defence minister, to try to get hold of Mnangagwa? Was it a genuine attempt to reach out to the former vice-president or a last-ditch effort to try to find him and bring him in? In retrospect, Collins is of the view that Mugabe may have agreed only to the dismissal of his father. He has strong doubts whether Mugabe then issued an order that his father be captured after he fled Harare. If Mugabe did not give the order that his former vice-president be apprehended, who in fact gave the instruction for Mnangagwa's arrest?

'I think that when the skirmishes were happening at the border, Mugabe did not know that and he did not sanction that. Someone triggered red alerts that Dad be arrested. When he [Mugabe] heard of the skirmishes he gave the instruction that whoever was at the border must be released. That's how Tarirai and Manzunzu were immediately released. They were just told that they could go now. A phone call came at the Forbes border post to the security officers that were there and then afterwards it was, We are done with questioning you, you can now leave and go. Just like that.'

If Collins's hypothesis is true, it may have been the G40 faction that put out the order in an effort to consolidate their newfound victory. The G40 faction was prepared to go to extreme lengths in respect of Mnangagwa and his allies, so long as it put them a few steps ahead in the long-drawn-out Zanu-PF succession contest.

* * *

At about 11.30 p.m. Mnangagwa was dropped off and joined his sons as they prepared to cross over into Mozambique at Marymount. The group had two vehicles. Mnangagwa was put inside a gold Mazda Demio while another car went ahead in pitch-black darkness, as the military intelligence personnel who provided safe passage indicated that none of the cars must have any of their headlights switched on.

For about fifteen kilometres, they drove in darkness to the crossing point. The slow drive felt like eternity, with frequent stops to make sure that they were not being followed or running into any security checkpoints.

While inside the car, Collins told his father of the call he had received from Sekeramayi's son on behalf of his father. Mnangagwa praised Collins for not disclosing that they were together.

The group arrived at the crossing point and everyone alighted from the vehicles. Mnangagwa had his brown Louis Vuitton briefcase by his side.

'The people that crossed with him at that point were three military personnel, Sean, Mavoro and Emmerson Jnr,' says Collins. 'I remained behind and was told to stay with the cars in case they found trouble up ahead and a quick exit was needed.'

At about 11.55 p.m., the group crossed the border and dashed into the no man's land that separates Zimbabwe and Mozambique. There they began the long journey of about thirty kilometres into Mozambique, walking in mud as it had rained. Danger continued to lurk, and often they had to take cover and hide from soldiers patrolling the territory. Eventually the mission was a success although it involved having to crouch down to avoid detection and it set the group back about $4 000 as they had to pay their way through. Once they arrived at the pickup point in Mozambique, a vehicle was on standby ready to collect Mnangagwa, his son and Mavoro. It then took them to Beira, where a plane collected them and took them to South Africa.

Told to wait by his father, Collins remained in the vehicle until 12.45 a.m., waiting for his twin brother, Sean, to return. When he finally got back, Sean could pass on the good news that their father had made it across into Mozambique. Relieved that they had been successful, the two brothers drove off to a service station where they slept for the rest of the night.

At daybreak, they headed back to Harare. To their surprise the drive back was without any incident and they were not stopped by police on the road. Collins went to Helensvale, where for the next two weeks, while their father was away in exile in South Africa, he stayed with his mother and looked after her. 'We were just the two of us. Nobody came to be with us during that time,' he says.

5

Help me, please

Almost two hours late, I finally arrive at the offices of the IT company Big Time Strategic Group, in Lynnwood Glen in Pretoria East, near Menlyn Mall, for what was supposed to have been a lunchtime meeting with its founder, Justice Maphosa, a Zimbabwean-born businessman who lives in South Africa. As a rule, I do not arrive late for appointments. But I am disappointed that I am nearly two hours late today and wonder whether Maphosa will still meet me.

My flight from Harare to Johannesburg had been perfectly planned. I would have left Harare at 7 a.m. and arrived in Johannesburg at 8.45 a.m. But when I got to Robert Gabriel Mugabe International Airport that morning, I was informed that the flight had been delayed. It would only depart at 10.30 a.m. It was not until 11 a.m. that Air Zimbabwe flight number UM462 finally took off for Johannesburg. Although no official reason was given by the airline's management for the four-hour delay, it later became clear what the reason was – or, rather, who the reason for the delay was. The captain announced that on board was former president Robert Mugabe. This was remarkable, as Mugabe had never been known to use commercial flights for foreign trips. Often, he preferred to charter a plane for himself rather than travel with ordinary citizens. Given Mugabe's past notoriety, I consoled myself with the thought that at least the flight had not been cancelled, which would have resulted in my missing my appointment completely.

But once inside the offices of Big Time Strategic Group, I quickly forget the morning drama. I am led to one of the boardrooms where I am advised that Maphosa will join me soon.

In a light blue jacket and a striped tie, Maphosa finally enters with two small phones in his hand. A firm handshake is exchanged between us. But before he takes his seat at the head of the table, Maphosa's eye is caught by a faulty lock on the door. He excuses himself and returns with someone whom he instructs to make sure it is fixed by tomorrow. It is this small incident before our conversation begins that suggests Maphosa is a stickler for detail, as I realise better later on.

Finally, Maphosa takes his seat. I am keen to get our conversation under way, partly because I feel guilty over the lost time following my delayed arrival.

Despite my being late, Maphosa is still accommodating and laughs at the reason why I was delayed and could not join him for lunch. Had it been he on the same flight, Maphosa says he probably would have gone to greet Mugabe as he still has great respect for the former president. He laughs out loudly. But he also quickly admits that the situation would have been extremely awkward because it was he who assisted Mnangagwa for the sixteen days in November 2017 when he was forced into exile in South Africa. Maphosa sheltered and protected Mnangagwa from the time that he fled to South Africa until his return on 22 November 2017 to take over as leader of the ruling party and the country.

Just like many Zimbabweans who live abroad, Maphosa had been following political events back home closely. He was aware of both the heightened political tensions in Zanu-PF caused by the succession question and the economic meltdown inflicting untold damage on the country. Maphosa had, however, never imagined that he would play a central role in the events of November 2017 that ultimately reconfigured Zimbabwe's political landscape. 'I never thought that I would be a key player. I never thought that I would be involved in politics, but I ended up being involved in the political situation by rescuing him [Mnangagwa]. By doing that, one was already saying, I have chosen a side, because there were two factions, you had G40 and Lacoste. So rescuing him meant that I was already seen as Lacoste. There was already that paralysis of a country divided into two; those that were pro the status quo and then those that were liberals like us who were saying, We are children of Zimbabwe and we want what's best for our country.'

In particular, Maphosa's interest in the political events of the country increased during the Presidential Youth Interface rallies held in 2017. It was at these rallies that Grace Mugabe often launched scathing attacks on Mnangagwa and humiliated him publicly. Maphosa has great admiration for Mnangagwa, for not buckling under the pressure brought to bear on him by Grace.

'For me, I thought that there is a leader being put through the fire. He was being put on the stage and humiliated so that he could then later be uplifted. That moment of being insulted was for his eventual elevation. It was the moment of character-building and self-preservation. It was the moment where he had to show how a leader remains under control amid the storm.'

* * *

The ruling Zanu-PF party was scheduled to hold its conference in Gwanda in December 2017. But by early October, it seemed increasingly likely that the annual Zanu-PF conference would not be just another uneventful week-long jamboree. Four provinces, Bulawayo, Midlands, Mashonaland West and Matabeleland South, were keen to turn the conference into an extraordinary elective congress, so that a new party leadership could emerge.

The Zanu-PF party congress is held once every five years and in principle it allows delegates to vote for a leader of their choice to take over the running of the party. The last party congress was held in December 2014, with the next one scheduled to take place only in 2019. That the ruling party was prepared to bring forward its elective congress by two years exposed the ongoing volatility that had gripped Zanu-PF. It simply could no longer continue on the path of pretending that all was well.

The congress would also, to an extent, provide an opportunity for a bare-knuckle fight to occur between the two rival factions, Lacoste and G40. Each faction would attempt to rally support and ensure victory for its own preferred candidate and, in the process, push out opponents. Publicly, however, the ruling party downplayed the significance of the call for an extraordinary congress. The party's secretary of administration, Ignatius Chombo, said the congress would allow Zanu-PF to prepare for elections in 2018 and also to 'tidy up' its internal affairs. 'On account that the last Congress, which ushered us into this session, was held in 2014, a lot has happened in the party. A lot of people were removed due to their alliances with [former vice-president Joice] Mujuru and her cabal. But critically, next year's election will be the first time that we will be using a new voters' roll, which is being worked out using the Biometric Voter Registration system – a totally new concept, which we did not have in the past. And it also means the old voters' roll has been destroyed and is no longer valid, so the whole country has to register anew. This coming year voters' rolls will be polling-station-based and these are all new developments. So, a lot of people were of the opinion that we need an Extraordinary Congress to look at all these developments and tidy up so that come 2018, we are all in the know as to what is going to happen and what the problems we could face are. But the Constitution has also changed and some people who were ineligible to vote in the past are now eligible to vote because they were born from parents one of whom was non-Zimbabwean. Now, the [Republic's] Constitution has a provision stating that all those people must be allowed to vote. So, all this has created a situation where others felt it would be better to have an Extraordinary Session of Congress to deliberate on these matters.'

Lying hidden beneath Chombo's comments, however, was the power struggle between warring factions in Zanu-PF. This had blown up hardly three years after the party's last vicious internal fight, which had resulted in the expulsion of Joice Mujuru at the 2014 congress. The gathering of about eight thousand delegates in congress had the potential to bring about a seismic shift in the leadership of the ruling party. In particular, the Lacoste faction was straining to have the party conference turned into an elective congress, as provinces such as the Midlands and Masvingo where Mnangagwa enjoyed support were agitating for his elevation to power.

On the other hand, the rival G40 faction was united in its opposition to this attempt. Instead, it favoured pushing on ahead with the gathering as a party conference. The main reason for its resistance to turning the annual event into an elective congress was that it was unsure whether Mugabe would win an election nomination unanimously to lead the deeply fragmented party. At ninety-three years, nature was not on Mugabe's side, and it was unimaginable that the party would win an election race on the back of a candidate of such an advanced age.

Had Mugabe not spoiled the Lacoste faction's plans to challenge him at the annual congress in December by firing Mnangagwa as deputy in government and party in early November, it is likely that the veteran ruler would have met a surprising end at the annual gathering. There, Lacoste had prepared for its supporters to vote for Mnangagwa against Mugabe in order to show the long-time leader the exit door.

A combination of factors was already stacked against Mugabe, strengthening Mnangagwa's hand. Mugabe was old and frail, and his wife had made it clear that she harboured ambitions to take over from him. These realities inspired little confidence that voters would be won over by a nonagenarian Mugabe and the prospect of a sharp-tongued Grace Mugabe at the helm. Tough decisions had to be taken and, with the benefit of military support – widely viewed as the country's king-makers – Mnangagwa was the favourite to take over the leadership of Zanu-PF and thus ensure the party's survival beyond Mugabe.

Maphosa confirms that Mnangagwa was the favourite to succeed Mugabe and that the annual gathering in December would have been used as a platform to mobilise and guarantee his support. Mnangagwa had popular support among the party provinces and had earned huge swathes of public sympathy from both the poisoning attempt in August 2017 and the persistent attacks from Grace Mugabe. He also had the confidence of the business community at home and abroad and was widely regarded as a seasoned politician who had served by Mugabe's side for over four decades.

'The only thing left was for them to go to congress, elect him and then he comes back and succeeds President Mugabe. But he was fired. For some of us we were filled with despair when that happened and we asked ourselves what's going on. It was a moment that left us to wonder about what's next and we started thinking that there was going to be a war in the country now because the mood was so tense on the ground and the resistance was huge.'

* * *

On the day that Mnangagwa was fired by Mugabe as Zimbabwe's vice-president, Maphosa received a phone call while he was still at the office from Mnangagwa's son Emmerson Jnr at around 6 p.m.

'Uncle, it's Junior. My father wants to speak to you.'

'Give the phone to your father so that I can speak to him,' he replied.

'Hello, comrade, how are you?' the former vice-president said at the other end of the line. 'Look, Maphosa, events have unfolded and I'm sure you are watching the news. I have been fired and I have been stripped of my bodyguards and I am now on the run. I'm going to try and find a way to run away from this, but it's very hot and I need your help.'

Maphosa immediately offered to assist. But what Maphosa was unaware of at the time was that Mnangagwa had already tried unsuccessfully to leave the country. Close associates had refused to assist him and his attempt to leave on medical grounds had failed to result in a swift response. The country's border posts were also on high alert.

'Keep your phone on,' Mnangagwa said. 'I will call you again in two hours because I am on the run. I will call you with a more secure line.'

Immediately after the conversation, Maphosa put together a rescue plan with his team of white security officers at his office, who he boasts are highly skilled and professional. Under Maphosa's direction a plan was hatched to track Mnangagwa's possible movements based on the phone call that he had just made and to estimate how long it would take him to reach a suitable pickup location. The plan was to collect Mnangagwa using Maphosa's private plane from Beira in Mozambique and to land at Lanseria Airport near Johannesburg. A second plane was on standby in the event that an emergency situation developed and the rescue plan ran into trouble in Mozambique.

'I did all this planning in order to prepare myself, so that in case I lost them I knew where I could begin to hunt for them,' says Maphosa. 'That was the next thing that I was going to do; if we lost him, we were going to send a search party to go and look for him. We wanted our president alive. We were prepared to go to Mozambique and look for him if we had lost him.'

For Maphosa, the acts of bravery during Zimbabwe's liberation war, when ordinary people often took on huge personal risks to provide food and shelter to guerrilla fighters, came to mind at the time. It was this sense that he was contributing to a mission of liberation that was much larger than himself that emboldened Maphosa to involve himself in the extremely dangerous operation of providing assistance to Mnangagwa. There were plenty of risks attached. One was that the authorities in Mozambique could raise the alarm that Mnangagwa was in the country to their counterparts in Zimbabwe. The authorities in South Africa could also make a move against Maphosa once their intelligence and surveillance systems picked up information that he was sheltering Mnangagwa from the government in Zimbabwe. Maphosa's involvement could also have invited the wrath of Mugabe and might even have soured relations between the three countries in the region.

It was because of all these associated risks that Maphosa decided not to inform his wife, when he arrived home in the early hours of Tuesday morning, that he was at the centre of an operation to assist Mnangagwa. As he got into bed, Maphosa held his wife closely and pretended that all was normal. 'My wife didn't know anything. I had not told her and I had made a decision that I was not going to tell her. This was too dangerous to discuss with my wife. If I had told her, she would have been fighting for her husband, whereas her husband had now found a new mission in life. She might have seen this as too dangerous and I can tell you 100 per cent that we would have ended up not doing it, because her input would have counted and she would have persuaded me not to go ahead with this. She would have raised certain concerns which I already had, but I was suppressing them because there was a need to do greater good out of this.'

So well kept was Maphosa's secret from his wife that she did not know that he was involved in assisting Mnangagwa until she saw the former vice-president at her doorstep days later in the company of her husband.

On the run, Mnangagwa meanwhile communicated with Maphosa at two-hour intervals. Different mobile phone handsets and numbers were used to keep in touch and these were quickly discarded as a safety precaution to prevent bugging or being tracked down by Zimbabwe's state security agents.

After the last call, which he received around 10 p.m., Maphosa did not receive any more from Mnangagwa. Although worried by the absence of communication, Maphosa went to bed with all his mobile phones switched on, hopeful that contact would be made soon.

At about 1.30 a.m. the next call from Mnangagwa came in, and he informed Maphosa that he had crossed over into Mozambique and was headed for Beira.

'Good shot. I know what to do from here. Find any disguise that you can and do whatever you can, but get to the airport.'

A deeply religious man, Maphosa says it would have been impossible to see through the rescue operation of Mnangagwa without God's intervention. 'Mozambique was aware that Mnangagwa was in the country. Anyone who claims they did it in their own power, they are lying. You would not have done this thing if God was not involved. It's all very simple: Zimbabwe could have called Mozambique and said, We have a fugitive; find him, catch him and bring him to us. The two countries have very good relationships and from president to president, and this could have been done easily.'

Although Maphosa was unwilling to go into specific detail, it seems that Mnangagwa and his entourage arrived at the airport in Beira in disguise. This made it difficult for the Mozambican authorities to recognise him.

At 6 a.m., Maphosa dispatched his plane from South Africa to Beira where it would pick up Mnangagwa and his sons. It was the beginning of yet another nerve-racking episode. There were delays to the paperwork for the plane, and this fuelled the fear that Mozambique was using delaying tactics.

'The clearance took a long time to come. I was worried why and I was thinking during that time of waiting that perhaps they were busy conveying information to the Zimbabwe government. The issue I was now faced with was, Do I dispatch a second plane and do I physically go there myself? It was a very tense moment and I kept on talking to the pilots to find out what was happening. The excuses for delay were petty reasons such as the manager on duty was not around.'

But finally, after a twelve-hour wait, the plane left Beira at 6.15 p.m. and headed for South Africa.

6

Hello, my president

Far from enjoying a close relationship with Mnangagwa, Maphosa can count the number of times that he had previously met and spoken to him before he received the call for help on the day that Mnangagwa was fired as Zimbabwe's vice-president. 'We were not close enough to do something like this. To do something like this, you had to do it with someone that you know,' says Maphosa.

But desperate, running out of options and with his back against the wall, Mnangagwa turned for help to Maphosa, who at that time was as good as a stranger. It was a moment in his life when Mnangagwa had to depend on other persons for his survival, including his sons. They took the decision to leave the country at great personal risk by accompanying their father to Beira. Along the way, they also had to act as his protectors. But once in South Africa, Mnangagwa had to rely solely on Maphosa. He had only Maphosa's word that he would help him, as promised during their initial phone call. There were no guarantees that Maphosa would stay true to his word or might not buckle under the pressure that could be brought to bear on him. Should word leak out that Maphosa was taking care of Mnangagwa, there was no telling what offers could be dangled before Maphosa by the authorities in exchange for Mnangagwa.

That Mnangagwa found a plane waiting to collect him in Beira, as

Maphosa had promised, gave him the earliest proof that he could confide in and trust the man. Ensuring his safety in South Africa would be the next hurdle for Maphosa, and once again Mnangagwa was able to rely on his host to see him through those dangers.

At about 7.45 p.m., after a flight of one and a half hours, Maphosa's private plane landed at Lanseria Airport near Johannesburg. Inside, Mnangagwa was one of the passengers.

Maphosa was aware of the dangers of his plan from the time the plane took off from Beira. The passenger was a high-profile Zimbabwean politician who travelled on a diplomatic passport. That alone could easily trigger all sorts of unwanted attention. There was also the possibility of the South African government becoming involved and even handing Mnangagwa over to the Zimbabwean authorities should Pretoria be approached by Harare.

'We had managed to survive Mozambique, but now South Africa was going to be an inferno. For starters, Mozambique might have missed him because they are not as electronically savvy as we are. However, in South Africa everything is electronic; your passport is scanned, your iris is scanned and your temperature is scanned to see if you should come in or you should not come in. A lot of things had already happened along the way. To complicate matters, we are talking about someone who was carrying a diplomatic passport entering into South Africa. These diplomatic passports raise alarm bells and are not like normal passports like yours and mine.'

To try to avoid detection, Maphosa had thirty identical black Range Rover SUVs, which were on the tarmac ready to scoop up Mnangagwa once he disembarked from the plane. The plan was to create a diversion, so that should any persons be watching their movements, they would be unable to identify which vehicle Mnangagwa had entered.

The scheme for Mnangagwa's rescue was devised by Maphosa and his security team during planning sessions held at the offices of Big Time Strategic Group. They were carefully thought through, as the margin of error had to be zero, but there was no guarantee everything would work out. One particular problem that occurred was that just before the plane landed, the police insisted that there were too many vehicles blocking the road. Maphosa could not openly inform the police why there were so many vehicles in attendance and who it was that they were collecting from the airport, without attracting unnecessary attention.

'Our mission was such that we also had to minimise the distance which Mnangagwa had to walk from the plane into the car,' Maphosa says. 'We didn't want him to move, mix and mingle with everyone else. Our intention was to steal him, put him in the car and drive away. We didn't want passers-by to realise that Emmerson was right there.'

Fortunately, at the immigration booth, the diplomatic passport that Mnangagwa holds did not raise any suspicions among the South African authorities. Mnangagwa walked off freely. But unbeknown to Maphosa and his convoy, while the flight from Beira was still in mid-air, the authorities in Mozambique informed their South African counterparts that Mnangagwa was en route to South Africa. Police were consequently on the lookout for a plane from Mozambique, but there had been some delay in the tip-off. This caused the police to think that the plane they were waiting for had not yet landed. In fact, it had already arrived.

'The plane that actually was carrying Mnangagwa was the plane that police were on the lookout for, but they were thinking it's not this plane. He was taken out by my bodyguards who are white men and who were wearing civilian clothes.'

As all this was happening, Maphosa was seated in his car observing from a distance. 'I am sitting in the car and I am watching all of this because I figured that I am a known figure. If I step in there, as I am known to be flying in there every day, and then these guys [police] see Maphosa, they will want to come and chat with me and thereby disturb me from my mission.'

Even when the convoy of thirty vehicles finally left the airport after

Mnangagwa had passed through immigration without incident, the police were still on the lookout for a plane from Mozambique.

After exiting from Lanseria, the convoy split into different directions. Almost immediately, one group that included some of Maphosa's bodyguards was stopped by the police and asked if they knew of a plane that had just landed from Mozambique. When the bodyguards pretended that their plane had come from Swaziland, they were allowed to proceed.

According to Maphosa, who was travelling in a black BMW X5 M-Badge, 'We decided to do this mission in different ways. We decided we will take many cars and keep playing on the road; one car will move, another will overtake and others will slow down and be overtaken. It was done so that the car in front would end up being at the back. We have too many X5s that look the same and too many Range Rovers that look the same and we had taken the number plates off all of them.

'The first four cars in front deliberately took off at high speed, so that anyone who might be following us would chase after those cars first. The first four cars had instructions to do between 180 and 200 km per hour and to drive for another 30 kilometres. The idea was to see who would pick up speed and follow. Those that were behind would accelerate and block them. We could do that; we could just block the road and allow our guys to escape.'

Once the convoy had left the airport behind, they enjoyed an uninterrupted ride. The X5 M-Badge in which Mnangagwa was being chauffeured, along with his son Emmerson Jnr, drove all the way at a comfortable speed until it reached its destination, a safe house in Pretoria.

'When we were just about to reach Pretoria, we found a lot of policemen on the road. However, they were conducting routine roadblocks. Paranoia got to us: I suppose only the guilty are afraid. I was thinking, This is a roadblock and we will be searched. But fortunately, because we were driving very slowly, we were not stopped and we got to where we were taking Mnangagwa.'

As the mission proceeded smoothly and the convoy finally reached the destination, the first words were exchanged between Mnangagwa and Maphosa.

'Hello, my president,' said Maphosa.

These three words broke the silence in which the four occupants of the vehicle had driven all the way from the airport terminal building – a silence reflecting the tenseness and risks of the situation. Maphosa knew well that should anything go wrong, not only would it mean great trouble for him and his security team, but it would spell danger for Mnangagwa too. But when they arrived at the safe house, he felt he could at last breathe freely, confident that he had managed to pull off his bold plan. At last feeling in full control of the situation, he spoke to Mnangagwa: 'Now we are here and we are going to look after you. You have got to trust me and I have got to trust you. In this situation, both of us have got to trust each other.'

* * *

After their arrival, Maphosa and Mnangagwa did not speak very much. Maphosa decided that he would address Mnangagwa as president as a way of reassurance that, despite the recent turn of events involving his dismissal, he still looked up to him and respected him as his leader. He recalls that Mnangagwa initially appeared subdued during their first meeting and seemed to be trying to come to terms with what had happened. When he got to the safe house, Mnangagwa refused to eat anything.

'He had a lot to process; it was obviously a new environment and he was put in this place, in this house where there were lots of body-guards guarding him both outside and inside. The bodyguards were white people and he didn't know what to expect from them. He obviously had fears and must have been thinking that maybe they would sell him out or someone will reveal his whereabouts. By and large he was a sitting duck and there was a lot for him to consider.'

Outside the room that Mnangagwa occupied in the safe house there were two armed bodyguards. All the windows and curtains in his room were kept closed. The only electronic gadget that was switched on was the air-conditioning unit. A supply of T-shirts, pyjamas, shirts, trousers and shoes had been made available for his use. No one was allowed entry into the room without permission from Maphosa.

Keen to ensure that Mnangagwa was secure and comfortable, Maphosa decided that he would also remain in the safe house. He left in the middle of the night to go home, where he spent a few hours before returning. Unaware that her husband was sheltering Mnangagwa elsewhere, Maphosa's wife was told that he was working on a project, so as not to raise her suspicions about his prolonged absence from home.

Next morning, feeling much more settled and in a better frame of mind, Mnangagwa narrated in detail to Maphosa over breakfast what had happened to him: how Mugabe had fired him, the tip-off he had received about the plot to arrest and kill him, and the journey by road to flee the country.

During their breakfast Maphosa once again reassured Mnangagwa that he was loyal to him and available to assist in any way that was needed. 'President, I am your servant and I am here to do this [protect you] and I will do it to the best of my knowledge. But there are certain things that I will say that we are not going to do now, so please work with me; it does not mean disrespect, it means that in this environment you are in our hands now and I know what's best. We have to work together; at certain places and at certain times we will not be able to go. Maybe certain things that you want us to do we will have to say to you it's dangerous and we can't do it, not now.'

The first request that Maphosa made to Mnangagwa was that he hand over all electronic gadgets that he might have in his possession, in particular any mobile phones. 'Anything that is electronic that you have must go; all the iPads and any tablets.'

It was only with time that Maphosa and Mnangagwa began to bond.

Maphosa fondly described the relationship that developed between them as one between a father and a son. They began to work together as a team, laughed together and spent time together in prayer.

With his experience of the political environment in South Africa, Maphosa put aside his normal work routine so that he could be by Mnangagwa's side and assumed the role of his personal aide. His tasks involved setting up meetings for Mnangagwa, ensuring that he had access to phone calls, and also debriefing him on the developments in Zimbabwe, as Mnangagwa was cut off from all forms of communication.

Although initially Mnangagwa had been confined to his room in the safe house, as trust grew and his safety was no longer considered to be under threat, the restrictions around him were relaxed.

While in South Africa, Mnangagwa went to meetings with persons whose names Maphosa refuses to disclose. Most of these meetings were held in private settings and away from the public eye. Security was a top priority whenever Mnangagwa travelled, with armed security accompanying him.

'There was even a stage where we felt we were being watched. You know, paranoia kicks in, and at one time we were planning to take him to my farm. My only worry about taking him to my farm, where I have two five-bedroom houses, is that there were Zimbabwean workers there. I figured out that they would know him and identify him and the word would leak out very fast that Mnangagwa was under my care.'

For Maphosa, the reality of what he was involved in struck him each time they were on the move with Mnangagwa. He is unwilling to disclose how they managed to move Mnangagwa about without anyone noticing him. It seems that disguises were a feature of Mnangagwa's stay while he was in exile in South Africa.

Maphosa believes that without God's intervention it would have been impossible to keep Mnangagwa alive and secure during his stay in South Africa. 'I think that all that happened is a testimony that

God is sovereign, he does what he wants and no one can thwart his purposes.'

At the time that Mnangagwa was hiding in South Africa, his whereabouts baffled the authorities in Zimbabwe. Maphosa claims that so closely guarded was the secret that Mnangagwa was in South Africa that even President Jacob Zuma did not know that the former Zimbabwean leader was in the country. Speculation in the media about Mnangagwa's whereabouts often provided comic relief at the time. 'We heard some of you media guys say he had gone to China. What I would then do was to download news from various media outlets and bring it to him and say, This is what the media is saying. In fact, we had a team of people downloading these stories in real time and we would brief him about everything happening around him so as to let him take the right decision as the president.'

One problem that Maphosa mentions as a challenge during Mnangagwa's stay was the need to communicate by phone. Maphosa feared that through triangulation and voice recognition, Mnangagwa's location could be traced and any person keen to find him would be able to do so. 'He would be moved about 20 kilometres away from his current location, so as to prevent triangulation by service providers to locate him should anyone be listening in on the conversation. Communication was our biggest nightmare. With communication, we could win it or we could lose it, and however much we feared it, he had to communicate with the outside world,' Maphosa says.

'We began to buy him cheap phones that used no operating system and he would use one a day and discard it. The next day we would bring him another one. We kept changing also where we were communicating from, so that if any people were tracking us, they would track us to a garage or to a busy mall. If they used the method of triangulation, the cellphone company would pinpoint a tower located in a busy mall, but no one would know where exactly we were if we were being tracked.'

Being in exile and away from home, Mnangagwa's mind was constantly on his family whom he had left behind in Zimbabwe. Sometimes, he would open up and speak of his concern for their safety, wondering whether they were safe and praying they would not be victimised by Mugabe.

Back home, developments began to unfold quickly. There was the warning by General Constantino Chiwenga that Mugabe should stop the purges in Zanu-PF. Subsequently army tanks rolled into Harare and Major-General Sibusiso Moyo announced that the military had taken over. Mnangagwa followed all these events very closely. But Mugabe's refusal to give way and the long, drawn-out negotiations that followed only heightened anxieties. Being so far from events on the ground made it even more difficult to deal with them.

'We were tense and it was not a celebration for us, but the firing of warning shots. The wolves could still come out in numbers and a lot of things could still go wrong. The army could revolt, break into two parts, and the people within our camps could also sell us out.'

Mugabe's stubborn refusal to step down also raised concern that the longer he dug in, the more fluid the situation could easily become, with no telling what the outcome might be. 'The longer Mugabe resisted, the more panicky the situation could become. What made it even more difficult is that we were sitting in South Africa and were not in Zimbabwe. In politics, an hour is a long time and your best friends could turn out to be your worst enemies in a short space of time. We all knew that Mnangagwa had to go back to Zimbabwe and become president. What we didn't know was how this would happen.'

I asked Maphosa, who had spent over two weeks with Mnangagwa and had developed a rapport with him, what he thought had finally sealed Mugabe's fate. After a brief pause to gather his thoughts, Maphosa insisted that the trouble began when ambition for power overran personal relationships. 'What business did he [Mugabe] have of wanting to put his wife as president to succeed him? The people around him were ill-advising him and he was listening only to things that he wanted to hear. Mugabe wanted music that only he loved to hear played in his ear.'

7

A father's daughter

'Ooh vana vangu', or 'Ooh, my children'. These were the first words that Emmerson Mnangagwa uttered when he saw his youngest daughter, Tariro, whom he endearingly calls 'my little one', by his hospital bedside. Tariro was in the company of her sister when they walked together into his hospital room at the Wits Donald Gordon Medical Centre in August 2017.

The two sisters had flown to Johannesburg two days after their father had been taken severely ill with suspected poisoning at a Presidential Youth Interface rally in Gwanda, some 160 kilometres south-west of Bulawayo. He was then airlifted to a military hospital in Gweru and from there flown to Johannesburg on the instruction of General Constantino Chiwenga after his condition had deteriorated sharply.

Anxious about the state of their father's health, the two sisters decided to visit him in South Africa and check on his progress. Their visit was supported by other family members, who helped pay for their flights. Besides being an opportunity for the two girls to see their father in person, the trip would enable anxious family members to get a first-hand account of how he was on their return.

'We got there and he was recovering and resting, but it turns out that he knew that we were coming to South Africa,' Tariro says. 'As soon as we crossed immigration at the airport in Harare, the intelligence told him that his two girls were leaving to go to South Africa. We got there Monday night, but it was too late to see him. We came on Tuesday morning; we got in and spent an hour with him. Then he said to take the next flight back and go back home and so we then came back. It was good for him to see us and for us also to be able to give a report-back to everybody else; that we have actually seen him and we were not just hearing from his doctors over the phone.'

The poisoning incident was for some a tipping point, the moment when the divisions within Zanu-PF became clear for all to see. In the aftermath of Mnangagwa's poisoning, suspicions ran high in the deeply fractured Zanu-PF party, and alarm bells sounded that the race to succeed Robert Mugabe could lead to dead bodies piling up along the way.

About forty-five minutes into Mugabe's address at the Presidential Youth Interface rally in August 2017, Mnangagwa stepped off the stage feeling unwell and was taken to a local clinic in Gwanda. Those that were closest to him at the time said he began vomiting uncontrollably and experienced slurred speech, loss of motor functions and balance, and severe diarrhoea. Two medical doctors who had travelled with him to the Gwanda rally, Sydney Sekeramayi and David Parirenyatwa, were by his side. According to family sources, the two doctors were of the opinion that it was essential to help stop Mnangagwa from vomiting. The medical staff in Gwanda received instructions over the phone from Mnangagwa's personal physician in Johannesburg about what to do to assist the patient.

His daughter Tariro tells me her father's poisoning may well have taken place before the start of the Gwanda rally. His feeling faint and the vomiting were merely manifestations of the poison already in his body.

At the time, media reports said Mnangagwa had boarded an air force helicopter at the Zimbabwe Defence College to travel to Gwanda. He was accompanied by Sekeramayi, the defence minister, and Parirenyatwa, the health and child care minister, who are both medical doctors by training. Airborne and en route to the rally,

Mnangagwa was reportedly served some samoosas, sandwiches and grapes.

'It was on the plane on the way to there [Gwanda] that he had grapes and samoosas,' says Tariro. 'Dad doesn't normally eat, because he knew of the threat that was there, but he just had a tiny grape. He said he took a small bite of the samoosas, but he didn't eat a lot of it because he doesn't like spicy food – he must have tasted the poison or whatever – then he took two pieces of grape.'

Another sister corroborates the story that their father had eaten some of the samoosa, which the family suspects was laced with poison. 'Imagine, just two bites and it took him down like that. What if he had eaten the whole thing?' the sister asked.

In January 2018, in his first interview with the international media after he had been inaugurated as Zimbabwe's third president, Mnangagwa told the London *Financial Times* that he knew who the people were that had administered the poison. 'I suspect as to who did it. They are still good friends of mine. I now suspect that they now know that I know,' he said.

In the interview, he also claimed that his doctors had identified the kind of poison he took: a rare hard metal arsenic toxin only available in Russia and Israel.

'They say it was an arsenic toxin, something like that, that's the class of poison and it's not easy to come round with it. They say it is colourless, it is tasteless and the areas where it could be found are possibly two ... Russia and Israel. So it's possible it came from Russia,' he said. 'They [the doctors] were surprised that I survived because I had a heart attack, what they call cardiac arrest ... So they kept me, you know, washing this out ... They have now declared that I am now OK. It's not visible anymore.'

The news of her father's poisoning reached Tariro through her young brother, Emmerson Jnr (not the same Emmerson Jnr who was part of the escape with their father to Mozambique), while she was at a nephew's first birthday party in Bulawayo. Her brother had received a phone call to tell him what had happened from one of his father's bodyguards.

How did she react to the report of her father suddenly being taken ill? The news was overwhelming, and Tariro remembers she just wanted to return to Harare but could not do so because of the party.

After she had calmed down, Tariro decided to inform the rest of her family. A deeply spiritual young woman, she views herself as the spiritual pillar of her family and encouraged everyone to pray for her father. 'We got news at some point that he was deteriorating and at some point I got everyone to come together at the farm, but on the way, as everybody was coming, things turned around and it began to be positive. So it ended up just being a thanksgiving time, we ended up praying and thanking God for his faithfulness. The concentration of poison in his blood was high and it's nothing short of a miracle that he is alive today,' she says.

Although her father survived the attempt on his life, the episode raised the already blazing political temperatures in the country. Supporters of Mnangagwa pointed an accusing finger at Grace Mugabe and the G40 faction. The G40 faction in turn tried desperately to dissociate itself from any perception that it was behind the foiled poisoning attempt. But in the eyes of the public, the episode tipped the scales in favour of Mnangagwa, who won widespread public sympathy for being the victim of what seemed to be a no-holds-barred effort by the G40 faction to elbow him out of the political succession race.

The Lacoste faction also used Mnangagwa's poisoning to score political points. A narrative began to emerge that Mnangagwa had eaten an ice cream from the Mugabes' dairy business, Alpha and Omega. In view of Grace Mugabe's show of anger at the suggestion that ice cream from her dairy business had been used to poison Mnangagwa, it seems the story had had real impact on the reputation and even perhaps the income of the Mugabes' business. To contain the damage, the information minister and government spokesperson, Christopher Mushohwe, issued a press statement in which he claimed that Mnangagwa had not eaten any ice cream at the Gwanda rally and insisted that any links between his illness and the ice cream were false.

Two days after Mnangagwa had fallen ill, Dr Parirenyatwa was quoted by the state-owned *Herald* newspaper as saying that the episode was nothing more than a severe bout of vomiting and diarrhoea. 'This is really to give an update to the country and the nation about the state of the Honourable Vice-President Mnangagwa's health. What I would like to say is that he has much improved. I have just spoken with him. He is quite jovial and he is well, really, but he requested, and we have sent him, to be seen by his doctors in South Africa where he is now. We are all aware that he had a severe bout of vomiting and diarrhoea in Gwanda and we took him to appropriate institutions within the country where he was properly stabilised and appropriate investigations were then commenced. We are still in progress to establish the source of that gastroenteritis or vomiting and diarrhoea. This is the situation. He is much better and well stabilised and, like I said, I spoke to him just now.'

* * *

A week before the Bulawayo rally of 4 November 2017 where Grace was booed and heckled by supporters of Mnangagwa, Tariro approached her father and told him that she wanted to attend.

'I went to Dad and I said to him, I want to come to the rally, I want to go to Bulawayo. But he said, No, I don't want you there because they are going to humiliate me. I said, What kind of humiliation that you haven't been through already? I want to be there. So he told me not to come, but my sisters and I decided that we wanted to go. My sister also saw him a day before the rally and said to him, We are going to be there, and he said, It's OK if that's what you have decided.'

Tariro drove from Harare to Bulawayo with her sisters Tasiwa and Chipo. When they arrived at White City Stadium they were surprised by the relatively low turnout of people at the rally. As it was Tariro's first time at a rally, she realised only then that TV producers tend to concentrate their cameras on sections of the audience with the largest number of people, to give the impression of a bumper crowd in attendance.

'Madame [Grace] then came onto the stage and she started spewing her nonsense. Then the booing started. I booed a little and then as more people began to boo, I also got more confident.' One of the members of their group took a video in which one could hear the booing voices. She sent it to a group on social media and it quickly went viral. 'At that point we were now freaking out because we did not know what was going to happen. The guy who was the chairperson of the Zanu-PF youth in Bulawayo, the one who died [Magura Charumbira], he was booing loudly and then there was a whole lot of fracas and he was pulled out of the crowd by the police.'

As Grace began her address, defending Jonathan Moyo, the crowds booed and shouted 'Mbava', which means thief, as she attempted to explain why Moyo should not be arrested. 'You know nothing' and 'You are too junior', other sections of the crowd shouted back. As the booing intensified, people chanted a popular song that is usually sung at football matches, 'Into oyenzayo siyayizonda', which means 'We hate what are you doing.'

Despite all these disruptions, Grace put on a brave face and continued with her address, standing her ground. 'If you have been paid to boo me, boo, go ahead, I don't care, I am powerful. Even if you bring soldiers to come and stand in front of me, I will not be afraid, I will continue to speak.'

If Grace tried to pretend that all was well at the Bulawayo rally, then her ninety-three-year-old husband did not attempt to hide his displeasure and anger at the situation. Mugabe deviated from his prepared speech and launched out against the crowd's behaviour, which he linked to supporters sympathetic towards Mnangagwa.

'Did I make a mistake in appointing Mnangagwa as my vice-president? If I erred, I will fire him by the end of day tomorrow. If he and his backers want to form their own party, so be it. We cannot have a party of friction and personal insults. Today when we have reached the tail end of the interfaces, we get all this nonsense. I don't like this. So, to the people in Masvingo with their attitude, you can go ahead and form your party because we honestly cannot have this. We cannot be insulted on a daily basis,' a fuming Mugabe said.

It was at the Bulawayo rally that Mugabe, who until then had attempted to play the role of unifier in the deeply divided Zanu-PF, finally showed his hand. By issuing the threat to fire Mnangagwa, instead of attempting to broker peace, it became clear that he was in the corner of the G40 faction.

Mugabe's iron fist, which had been hidden in a velvet glove, was now exposed, and all could see that he was intent on removing his deputy, whose supporters had openly booed his wife. The booing and heckling of Grace was a public embarrassment for someone who considered herself invincible. It was also personally stinging for Mugabe, who had watched his wife read the riot act to her political rivals during the previous three years. Tariro says that Mugabe was caught unaware by the open challenge to his wife in Bulawayo.

'Mugabe wasn't expecting that, and he is usually somebody who is composed, but he lost his cool and that's when he threatened to fire Dad. We left the stadium and then heard that he [Mugabe] was now at the airport and had sent soldiers to go and find every single person who was booing and bring them to him.'

* * *

When her father was fired by Mugabe two days later, Tariro woke up with a passage from Scripture in her heart that she wanted to share with him. She believed that the passage in question, about Saul's hatred for David, was significant and would explain the situation that her father was in. The biblical story is about the rejection of Saul as king of Israel and the approaching elevation of David as his replacement.

Feeling compelled to speak to him, Tariro went to his office at around 11 a.m., but as she was about to arrive, she saw him drive off. At that moment, she had no idea that he had already been fired as vice-president. Disappointed that she did not have the opportunity to speak to him, she consoled herself with the thought that she would see him later in the day. 'Then later on in the day in our family group chat, my sister Farai messaged to say that Dad has been fired and she said everybody must go home to his house in Helensvale. At that time my brother's car was being serviced and I was deciding on whether to go and pick him up, and then another sister also said she didn't have a vehicle. So I first went all the way to Tynwald to go get my brother and then went to pick up my sister, who had a small child and was taking a long time to get ready. Eventually, we got to Helensvale, but Dad was gone. He had left and this was around 6 p.m. I felt bad at the time because I was thinking that I had a word that I wanted to give him since morning. I totally broke down and it wasn't about him being fired or running away, but because I thought he needed to hear this word from God and I didn't tell him,' she says.

At the family home she found the rest of the family. Unable to do anything further, the family prayed together for the safety of their father and the sons who had accompanied him to the Forbes border post. They then all went to bed. The following day, the family was informed of the attempts by the police to prevent their father from crossing the border into Mozambique.

'We heard now the story of him having been grabbed by a police-man. I was like, How dare this little ZRP person put his hand on my father? He grabbed him apparently and we heard of gunshots that were fired and that a gun was placed at my brother's face, one of the twins,' she says.

Although relieved to hear that their father had finally been able to cross the border and was now safely in Mozambique, the family members left behind were closely watched by state security and had their phones tapped. The family caught wind of plans by members of the intelligence services to raid the family home in search of incriminating documents that showed Mnangagwa was disloyal to Mugabe and was planning a coup. Unwilling to take any risks, Tariro went to their family house in Tynwald and removed just about anything that she thought 'might be misrepresented into something that it was not by their father's enemies'.

She recalls that at the time her father had to flee, General Chiwenga was also away in China. The family, she says, felt vulnerable and exposed. 'You didn't know who to trust and how much you could say. Our phones were tapped and you could blatantly hear that somebody was listening in on conversations. Dad would call Farai, my eldest sister, for like two minutes and it was not for long. So we were all waiting for those moments to hear from him and to hear what he wanted to say.'

According to Tariro, so as to avoid having their conversations listened into, a third party would get in touch with her eldest sister, Farai, and instruct her to get a new handset and a new mobile number, and call a certain number. 'Once she did that, she didn't speak, I think they knew it was her and then they with another number would contact her. So very briefly the conversation with Dad was: How are you? I'm OK, how are the children doing? Do this and do that. OK, bye.'

Every second day this form of communication between Mnangagwa and his eldest daughter became the norm while he was in exile. He would tell her what she had to do and she would update him on developments on the ground.

Tariro says there was never any attempt to physically harm the family members that were left in Zimbabwe. However, in addition to being put under surveillance, family members who operated businesses had pressure applied on them by the authorities. Their bank accounts were frozen, presumably to prevent them from providing any financial assistance to their father in exile.

* * *

The relationship between Chiwenga and Mnangagwa is described as very close by Tariro. Consequently, she was little surprised when the army tanks rolled into Harare late in the afternoon of 14 November 2017, a day after Chiwenga had warned Mugabe to stop the purges in Zanu-PF. The army chief had warned that the sweeping purges within the ruling party had the potential to spark unrest in the country. The focus on the internal fights in Zanu-PF had become an albatross around the neck of the country's economy: its national leadership had become so deeply engrossed in scoring political points against each other that they had neglected to deliver on the economic promises made to voters. If it continued on the same path, Chiwenga warned, the ruling party would be heavily punished at the forthcoming elections.

The military intervention might perhaps have come sooner had Chiwenga not been sent away to China by Mugabe at the time of Mnangagwa's firing. It seems that Chiwenga's loyalty to Mnangagwa was never in doubt. He had been strategically removed from the ground by Mugabe, which made it nearly impossible for him to take any decisive action *in absentia*.

His return from China on 12 November 2017 and the attempt to arrest him at the airport only underscored the fear of the G40 faction that Chiwenga would deal decisively with the political bickering in Zanu-PF. Following his expulsion as vice-president, Mnangagwa was fired three days later from Zanu-PF. The net was cast wider and the intention was to purge as many of Mnangagwa's allies as possible and to weaken his Lacoste faction. Quoting an online report by the state broadcaster, the Zimbabwe Broadcasting Corporation, news agency Reuters said that Zanu-PF leaders in the eastern Manicaland region had called for the expulsion of cyber security minister Patrick Chinamasa, a former finance minister. Chinamasa, fellow cabinet ministers Oppah Muchinguri-Kashiri and Christopher Mushohwe, and thirty-six other party members and officials were accused of being Mnangagwa allies who were disrespectful of Mugabe. 'The province recommended the expulsion of 39 individuals who were involved with the Mnangagwa-aligned "Lacoste" faction, who is accused of not respecting the party's one centre of power principle,' the ZBC online report said.

For Tariro and her family, this was a deeply trying time. The family felt exposed in the absence of both their father and Chiwenga, who was not only loyal to their father but was essentially part of their family. 'He is a brother to Dad, I mean especially the way he came through for him in August [when Mnangagwa was poisoned] and we knew that he was the only person who had his back and also had it powerfully. So it's a very important and close relationship which goes back to when Mom was still alive as well. He [Chiwenga] would tell stories of when they were in Mozambique and when my sisters were younger and they were in Mozambique together with Dad. So it's a very close friendship and a very long friendship and the brotherhood is still there.'

For Tariro, the difficult times faced by the family in 2017 taught her vital lessons and helped her to realise whom she could count on. It is a lesson that she will carry throughout her life. 'During the poisoning saga and during the great escape into Mozambique, you really saw who was with you then. So even after Dad's inauguration in November last year, you knew the people to hang around with, those which have your back,' she says.

8

This is not a coup

In the office of one of the Western countries' ambassadors in Harare, my eyes gaze on a tin container on the table. The ambassador had asked not to be named and requested the meeting to be off the record.

On the tin container is a picture of a pipe and beneath it are the words 'Ceci n'est pas une pipe'. Perhaps noting that my attention had been caught by the object, my host picked it up and explained the meaning of the image. It is by René Magritte, a Belgian surreal artist, and the words inscribed below the image of the pipe mean 'this is not a pipe'. He gives a hearty chuckle and goes on to borrow the words of Magritte to sum up his thoughts about the events of November 2017 when Mugabe was forced to resign under military pressure. In a witty play on words, he tells me, 'This is not a coup.' Quickly, he adds: 'But in fact we all knew that it was a coup, it ticked all the boxes of a coup, but we deliberately also came together as the diplomatic community and agreed not to call it as such. We used the words "military intervention". I guess we also wanted to give this thing a chance to see where it would go.'

The term 'military intervention' was coined by the army to justify its actions in taking over the temporary running of the affairs of the country from Mugabe. It was first used by Major-General Sibusiso Moyo, who appeared on the national broadcaster in the early hours of 15 November to announce the military action that had occurred overnight. Moyo was subsequently included in Mnangagwa's new cabinet and appointed the foreign affairs minister.

The army deliberately used the term 'military intervention' to deflect and avoid the kind of condemnation that a coup could provoke from other countries in the region and internationally and, closer to home, the possibility of charges of treason being brought against them. Their careful choice of words was also meant to ensure that Mugabe's successor, Mnangagwa, would not be tainted by the charge of having come to power through orchestrating a coup. This concern for Mnangagwa's image appears to have paid off. In April 2018 he was listed as one of *Time* magazine's 100 most influential individuals.

But how is it that the fall of Mugabe at the hands of the military failed to elicit either condemnation of its actions or sympathy for the man from the Southern African Development Community and the international community? Beyond various press statements released by SADC and the African Union, there appeared to be a strong reluctance on their part to become involved in the affairs of November 2017. In part, the lack of sympathy for Mugabe's fall was of his own doing. Within the region he was the last of the founding fathers in SADC still in power. At ninety-three years old, Mugabe had ruled Zimbabwe for thirty-seven years but, despite his advanced age and increasing frailty, he was not showing any signs of slowing down. It seemed that his long stay in power bothered him little. At public gatherings he would often delve into the issue of his succession and vowed never to step down for as long as the people wanted him to stay on. By his side, his wife, Grace, echoed this stance and insisted that even if her husband's health deteriorated he would rule from the wheelchair, and, if he died, he would rule from beyond the grave. In fact, at the time of his fall, Mugabe had made himself available to stand for his eighth consecutive presidential contest in the 2018 elections.

Mugabe's stance was at odds with the prevailing situation in the rest of the region. Several countries in southern Africa had in different ways experienced winds of change within their borders in the final years of Mugabe's rule. New leaders had been sworn in in Zambia, Malawi, Tanzania, Namibia, Mozambique and Botswana.

While his continued stay in power was justified by his supporters as legitimate and unexceptionable, given that he had won open elections, the rest of the countries in the region were having to deal with the consequences of Mugabe's continuation in office and the impact of his country's economic ruin. For nearly two decades his neighbours had had to absorb a growing number of migrants from Zimbabwe, who had fled from the 'sick man of the region'. This can perhaps explain the reluctance of Zimbabwe's neighbours to assist Mugabe when the army took over power and pushed him out. Several regional diplomats expressed the commonly held feeling that Mugabe had stayed for too long and 'it was time for the old man to leave'.

Already in September 2016, Botswana president Ian Khama appeared to have had enough of the 'Mugabe problem'. He told Reuters news agency that Mugabe should step aside without delay and allow for a new leadership in Zimbabwe, as the country's political and economic implosion was dragging down the whole of southern Africa. At the time, Botswana was home to an estimated 100 000 Zimbabweans. Although this number is relatively small in comparison to the three million estimated to have taken refuge in South Africa, it was still large enough to strain the public services of Botswana, whose population is no more than 2.3 million people. 'Without doubt. He should have done it years ago. They have got plenty of people there [in Zimbabwe] who have got good leadership qualities who could take over. It is obvious that at his age and the state Zimbabwe is in, he's not really able to provide the leadership that could get it out of its predicament. It is a big concern. It is a problem for all of us in the region – and it is a burden. There's no doubt about that,' Khama said.

In 2017, as pressure mounted on Mugabe to step down, Khama repeated his call that the long-time ruler should leave office. 'I don't think anyone should be president for that amount of time. We are presidents, not monarchs. It's just common sense,' he said. Khama, who stepped down in April 2018 as Botswana's leader, attended the inauguration of Mnangagwa on 24 November. Other regional heads of state in attendance included Zambia's Edgar Lungu and Mozambique's Filipe Nyusi.

How Mugabe felt about being abandoned by his regional peers only became apparent when he spoke to the *Sunday Times* in March 2018 in an exclusive interview at his Blue Roof mansion in Borrowdale in Harare. Mugabe opened up about the disappointment and indeed betrayal that he felt at not receiving help from the region during his darkest hour. In particular, he singled out former South African president Jacob Zuma, who he said 'could have done more' to assist him. Zuma was the chairperson of SADC at the time of the army intervention. Mugabe said that Zuma instead had sent 'junior officials' who were biased and did not provide the South African government with an accurate report of their findings. The team dispatched by Zuma comprised the minister of defence and military veterans, Nosiviwe Mapisa-Nqakula, and the state security minister, Advocate Bongani Bongo.

'In a way I feel betrayed, but you have to also look at their conditions. Besides South Africa, most of them did not have the capacity to intervene. South Africa could have done more, but it didn't. They set a bad precedent. They [Zuma's special envoys] had come here, they had seen the situation and then they went to say there was no need for intervention. That is because they had spoken to the commanders. South Africa did not have to send an army, but to engage more. You see this group of ministers that came; they gave a false impression that all was OK and they had spoken, not just to us, but also to the soldiers. Now if they had spoken to soldiers and then gave out that there was no need for intervention because they had been assured, then the other countries just sat on their laurels and they said, Ah well, South Africa says there is no need. Afterward, when the situation became worse, they didn't want to change their original view,' Mugabe said.

Desperate and isolated, Mugabe went on an offensive to engage regional leaders one by one in an effort to enlist their help. He admits to having spoken to South Africa's former president Thabo Mbeki, Zambian president Edgar Lungu, Mozambican president Filipe Nyusi, Kenya's president Uhuru Kenyatta, and Jacob Zuma as he lobbied for help. No assistance was forthcoming. Flanked by his wife during the interview, Mugabe said he believed that there must have been a 'third hand' at play that had convinced the regional leaders not to step in.

* * *

On the international stage, Mugabe's fallout with the West was triggered largely by his disagreement in 1997 with Britain over Zimbabwe's land-reform programme. The former colonial master was accused by Mugabe of reneging on an agreement signed at Lancaster House in 1979 that it would pay compensation to white farmers for land acquired by the government and redistributed to landless blacks in Zimbabwe. The British government that had just come into power was led by Tony Blair.

Heidi Holland, the late author of the book *Dinner with Mugabe*, refers to Britain's diplomatic blunder over its about-turn on paying for land compensation, which she identifies as the start of the souring of relations between Harare and London. 'It was a letter written in 1997 by Britain's secretary of state for international development, Clare Short, that forced Mugabe to confront the fact that he was not after all omnipotent. She wrote it following a disagreement between Mugabe and Blair over Zimbabwe's land redistribution plans during a Commonwealth conference in Edinburgh, earlier that year. In it Clare Short dismissed Zimbabwe's contention that Britain had an obligation to fund land redistribution in the former Rhodesia. "I should make it clear that we do not accept that Britain has a special responsibility to meet the costs of land purchase in Zimbabwe," she said. "We are a new government from diverse backgrounds without links to former colonial interests. My own origins are Irish, and as you know, we were colonized not colonizers."'

Holland believes that Short's letter angered Mugabe intensely: 'The newly elected Labour administration was "worse than the Tories". It accounted in part for the Zimbabwean president's open hatred of Tony Blair a few years later.'

Ever the artful politician, Mugabe nevertheless used the fallout with Britain to project himself as a neocolonial fighter against Western imperialism. The West, personified by Britain, became Mugabe's new sworn enemy. His administration in turn adopted a 'Look East policy', which was meant to be a slap in the face for the West, at the time Harare's largest trade partner. China and Russia became Mugabe's new bosom buddies, as relations with the West deteriorated.

In an interview with the *Mail & Guardian* published on 30 January 2015, Didymus Mutasa, a former ally of Mugabe who was fired from Zanu-PF at its December 2014 congress, admitted that most of the policies under Mugabe were poorly thought out. He singled out the 'Look East policy' for failing to produce the envisaged returns as had been widely expected, when I asked if he had any regrets about his time in government. 'In a way, yes, we have taken away people's land and we are not making good use of those farms. When you see how many Zimbabweans are in South Africa, it's millions. What are they going there for? It's work. We draw up fantastic blueprints but with no money to achieve them. It makes me very sad. I have always wondered about our Look East policy, which confines Zimbabwe to Russia and China. You then see how faulty some of our policies are. You never think about them clearly and they are given to you in a memorandum, and when you meet your cabinet and Politburo colleagues to discuss them, you are told there is no time and we move to other issues.'

In retaliation, Western governments slapped sanctions on Mugabe, his wife and over a hundred senior members of Zanu-PF and the military in a bid to cripple his administration. But Mugabe still hung onto power and used the sanctions to draw sympathy for himself from other African states and cast himself as a victim of Western aggrandisement. In October 2013, the Zimbabwean government filed a lawsuit in the European Court of Justice in Brussels for losses to its economy arising from the impact of European sanctions on the country and asked for $42 billion in compensation. *Business Day* (24 October 2013) said the Zimbabwe government's contention was that sanctions imposed by the EU since 2001 had cost the country $42 billion in lost revenue. An EU representative at the time told the publication: 'The restrictions are against ten individuals and one company and not against the whole of Zimbabwe. There is no such thing as sanctions against Zimbabwe.'

In the last seventeen years of his rule, Western governments and in particular the US and UK bore the brunt of the tongue-lashing from Mugabe. Moreover, the West's perceived association with the opposition party, the Movement for Democratic Change, infuriated Mugabe and sent the state propaganda machine into overdrive. He vilified his political rival Morgan Tsvangirai as a puppet of the West and claimed that the West was engaged in sponsoring regime change in Zimbabwe.

* * *

By the time Mugabe's end came, there was neither sympathy nor a lifeline of support to cling to from his regional neighbours or from the international community. Mugabe had isolated himself. 'What we saw on 18 November on the streets by ordinary Zimbabweans in terms of the emotional outburst, mirrors to a large extent what the diplomatic community also felt at the time. There was strong relief,' says the ambassador whom I interviewed in Harare. 'We had really been frightened by the prospect that Grace was being positioned to take over power from her husband.'

The internal fights in Zanu-PF between the factions loyal to her and those loyal to Mnangagwa were closely followed in all their ferocity by the ambassador. With years of diplomatic experience under his belt, the ambassador had reached the conclusion that the sheer volatility of the situation in Zanu-PF made it impossible for Mugabe to remain at the helm. Working against him were such known factors as his old age, sickness and increasing frailty. The ruling party, which was facing elections in 2018, had achieved very little and had little to show for its performance. It was in fact staring down the barrel of a gun, confronted by the real prospect of voters turning against Zanu-PF at the polls.

'If I was a betting person, I would have bet and successfully won. But as early as August we had made the call that Mugabe would not be in charge of Zanu-PF by the time the country went into elections this year [2018]. What we did not foresee is how that would have happened,' the ambassador says. The military element also 'took them by surprise'.

Regardless of the surprise that the ambassador expressed, rumours have persisted in Harare that certain Western governments had advance knowledge of the army's action against its former commander-in-chief. On 15 November, at 2.19 a.m. on its Twitter feed, the US embassy in Zimbabwe was the first Western embassy in Harare to announce its closure. 'As a result of the ongoing political uncertainty through the night, the Ambassador has instructed all employees to remain home tomorrow. U.S. government personnel have been instructed to shelter in their residences tonight and work remotely from home on November 15. The embassy will be minimally staffed and closed to the public. U.S. citizens in Zimbabwe are encouraged to shelter in place until further notice. Please monitor news and embassy notifications.'

Other Western embassies followed suit and issued their own travel warnings. But it was the statement from the US embassy that gave the first and strongest indication that something was happening in Harare. In the absence of any credible information from the authorities in Harare, the US embassy announcement was the first reliable source of news that some seismic shift in power had happened.

I had stayed up all night scanning Twitter and social media platforms and spoke to various contacts to try to find out what was happening. I had also heard overnight explosions, but these had been muffled by the heavy downpour just after 1 a.m. In that moment, I even thought that my mind was playing tricks on me. Shortly after 3.30 a.m., I slipped into bed, but it was not for long. Alerted by a contact to watch a broadcast by the military on the national broadcaster, I was soon up again and seated in front of the TV.

At exactly 4 a.m. on 15 November, a military spokesperson, Major-General Sibusiso Moyo, appeared on TV and announced that the military was now temporarily in charge. His statement read:

> To both our people and the world beyond our borders, we wish to make it abundantly clear that this is not a military takeover of Government. What the Zimbabwe Defence Forces is doing is to pacify a degenerating political, social and economic situation in our country which if not addressed may result in violent conflict. We wish to assure the nation that His Excellency, the President of the Republic of Zimbabwe and Commander-in-Chief of the Zimbabwe Defence Forces, Cde R.G. Mugabe, and his family are safe and sound and their security is guaranteed. We are only targeting criminals around him who are committing crimes that are causing social and economic suffering in the country in order to bring them to justice. As soon as we have accomplished our mission, we expect that the situation will return to normalcy. To the generality of the people of Zimbabwe, we urge you to remain calm and limit unnecessary movement. However, we encourage those who are employed and those with essential business in the city to continue their normal activities as usual. Our wish is that you enjoy your rights and freedoms and that we return our country to a dispensation that allows for investment, development and prosperity that we all fought for and for which many of our citizens paid the supreme sacrifice. To the civil servants, as you are aware, there is a plan by the same individuals to influence the current

purging which is taking place in the political sphere to the civil service. We are against that act of injustice and we intend to protect every one of you against that. To the judiciary, the measures under way are intended to ensure that, as an independent arm of the State, you are able to exercise your independent authority without fear of being obstructed, as has been the case with this group of individuals. To our Members of Parliament, your legislative role is of paramount importance for peace and stability in this country and it is our desire that a dispensation is created that allows you to serve your respective political constituencies according to democratic tenets. To the youth, we call upon you to realise that the future of this country is yours. Do not be enticed with dirty coins of silver, be disciplined and remain committed to the ethos and values of this great nation. To all churches and religious organisations in Zimbabwe, we call upon you and your congregations to pray for our country and preach the gospel of love, peace, unity and development. To members of the Defence Forces, all leave is cancelled and you are all to return to your barracks with immediate effect. To our respected traditional leaders, you are the custodians of our culture, customs, traditions and heritage, and we request you to provide leadership and direction to your communities for the sake of unity and development in our country. To the other security services, we urge you to cooperate for the good of our country. Let it be clear that we intend to address the human security threats in our country. Therefore, any provocation will be met with an appropriate response.

The military intervention marked a decisive shift in the balance of power in Zimbabwe. The military's message to Zimbabweans, to the region and the rest of the world was concise: this was not a coup. In a report published in December 2017, the NGO International Crisis Group succinctly summarised the reasons why the military went to great lengths to ensure that their action was not labelled a coup.

Both then-Zimbabwe Defence Forces commander General Constantino Chiwenga and Mnangagwa claimed the military intervention was necessary to preserve the revolution and stabilise the country. Observers described it as a 'military-assisted transition', a fudge widely accepted both inside and outside Zimbabwe to avoid labelling it a coup, which would have triggered continental and international sanctions. It was spearheaded by elements of the security sector fearful of the rising influence within Zanu-PF of individuals threatening their political and economic interests. The overall acquiescence in their actions is understandable: it reflects fatigue with Mugabe and hope among Zimbabweans as well as external parties that the new rulers can reverse the country's calamitous economic decline. Still, the military's involvement sets a worrying precedent, raising questions about the role of opaque power-brokers …

The military were at pains to ensure a legal and constitutional veneer for their intervention given that a coup remains a red line for both the Southern African Development Community (SADC) and the African Union (AU), and would have resulted in sanctions, as well as sinking prospects for donor support. The military and its co-conspirators therefore needed Mugabe's acquiescence, which was his final bargaining chip. He refused to step down and a stand-off ensued as he attempted to cling to power as well as obtain guarantees for his family and key G40 members.

* * *

As news of Mugabe's fall began to spread around the world, international leaders gave their views on the developments in Zimbabwe. Generally, reactions from foreign governments were positive. In the UK, Prime Minister Theresa May said: 'The resignation of Robert Mugabe provides Zimbabwe with an opportunity to forge a new path free of the oppression that characterised his rule.' Britain's foreign secretary, Boris Johnson, said: 'I will not pretend to regret Mugabe's downfall: but this can now be a turning point, a moment of hope for this beautiful country, full of potential.' In the United States, a State Department spokesperson called it 'a historic opportunity, a historic moment for the people of Zimbabwe ... to put an end to Zimbabwe's isolation', adding that 'the future of Zimbabwe will have to be decided by the people of Zimbabwe'. The Chinese Foreign Ministry put out a statement that read: 'As a friendly country to Zimbabwe, we are closely following the situation unfolding in Zimbabwe. Zimbabwe's peace, stability and development serve the fundamental interests of the country itself and other regional countries. It is also the common wish of the international community. We hope that Zimbabwe could properly handle its internal affairs. As for the whereabouts of the former Vice-President of Zimbabwe [Mnangagwa], I can assure you that he is not in China.'

9

Trust no one

When her father was on the run, Farai Mlotshwa, Mnangagwa's eldest daughter from his marriage to his late first wife, Jayne, got a call at around 10 a.m. from a senior military officer in the Zimbabwe Air Force. The officer, whom she viewed as a friend, asked to see her. They met at the Mugg & Bean restaurant in the upmarket Sam Levy's Village in Borrowdale in Harare. But afraid that some harm might befall her and that she could even be kidnapped, she asked her sister Tapiwa to join her. Tapiwa, however, sat at an adjacent table at the restaurant and, from a distance, without the knowledge of the officer, kept a watch on their meeting.

The officer told Farai that they had lost track of her father, after his failed attempt with his sons to cross at Forbes border post. 'Some of our guys were following your father in terms of protection, but they have lost him. So we need to know where he is, because he is alone. He is just with the boys and our security guys can't see him.'

Farai is a former Zimbabwean diplomat to South Africa, where she served from 2006 to 2016. She says she has personally known the officer as far back as her days as an envoy and they are good friends. Although there was some level of trust between them, his request was hard to grant.

'How can I trust you?' Farai asked him. 'It's the state that's after my father, and you now want me to tell you where my father is?'

Calm and collected, he reminded her that they had known each other for a very long time and in all that time he had always been supportive of her father.

'I wouldn't lie to you and it is Perence Shiri [then commander of the Zimbabwe Air Force] who has sent me,' the officer told her. 'Your father needs our help and we can't let him be just with the boys. He needs help, otherwise they might kill him. They might get to him and we wouldn't be able to protect him.'

Torn between her desire to see her father protected and her suspicion about the genuineness of the offer to help, Farai got in touch through her husband, Gerald Mlotshwa, with her brother Emmerson Jnr, who was then at a hideout in the bush in Mutare and conveyed the officer's request.

'No no no, don't tell anyone where we are. They might send a platoon to finish us off. Trust no one,' was the emphatic response that came back from her brother.

When Farai told the officer, he insisted that she give him the information for the sake of her father's own safety. Mnangagwa's life was at stake, he said. Finally, Farai gave in and agreed to disclose her father's whereabouts, on condition that they travel together to his hiding place. 'I told him, If you are going to kill my father, the very least I can do is that I be there when you do it. You will have to do it in front of me,' she said. Only after he had got the green light from his supervisors did he agree to the terms she had laid down.

But just before they could set out for Mutare, the officer called and informed her that the trip was off. He told her that someone was following him and had listened in on their conversation; so their plan was known and they would be tailed on their way.

'Let's pray that nothing happens, but we are in communication with our guys at the border and so far there have been no further incidents,' he told her.

It is not clear if Mnangagwa knew that the military was watching and following from a distance, although they did not make direct contact with either him or his sons until much later. Where the military stood on the question of Mnangagwa's firing became apparent a week afterwards, when on 13 November General Constantino Chiwenga spoke out about the purges in Zanu-PF. The die had been cast, and it was clear that the military and its powerful generals were on Mnangagwa's side.

After Mnangagwa had crossed into Mozambique and was flown to South Africa, he first communicated with his eldest daughter only several days later. Their telephone conversations were usually very brief. He would ask after her, the children and the welfare of the rest of the family. During the first few days of his exile, their communication went via a third party. His doctor at the Wits Donald Gordon Medical Centre in Johannesburg was the contact person who would relay messages between father and daughter. It was also through his doctor that Farai sent a friend to drop off money for her father. His bank accounts had been frozen and so she gave her father R100 000. Another staunch ally chipped in with R50 000. 'I would also send handsets to him, those small ones,' Farai says. 'He had people that were giving him phones, but we didn't know who he was with. I didn't entirely trust those people either, because I didn't know who they were. So I sent with the doctor a handset to get to Dad and a sim card, which he didn't use. Apparently he was getting a phone and a new sim card every day anyway, but I didn't know that.'

While her father was exiled in South Africa, Farai was approached by the BBC, which asked for a radio interview with her. She agreed, on condition that the questions would be given to her in advance. She recalls that the interview proceeded smoothly and she received another interview request from the same broadcaster.

Although in hiding, Mnangagwa made a point of listening to news broadcasts out of Zimbabwe. When he heard about his daughter's interview with the BBC, he called her and asked that she 'stay away from the media'. His reasoning was that the media could try to bait her in order to get to him through the questions they put to her. She had a recording of the interview and played it over the phone for him, to reassure him that she had been measured and responsible in what she had said and also to defend herself in the event that she was misquoted.

Mnangagwa listened to the interview and commended her for answering the questions well. 'But please, no more interviews,' he said. 'They will keep pulling you in and I don't want you involved. If anyone gets hold of you, say, Speak to my father, I have no comment.'

That was the last media interview that she did.

How did she feel about her father being turned into a fugitive and exile after being the second most powerful person in Zimbabwe? I asked her.

Betrayal: that was what summed up Farai's feelings about the events of November 2017. She was angry with Mugabe, who had 'betrayed' her father. She insisted that her father had always been loyal to Mugabe, even to his own cost, and often would reprimand her whenever she criticised the president. 'Don't speak like that. We have come a long way together,' was what he would say to his eldest daughter.

Infuriated with Mugabe and angered by the way in which her father had been humiliated, she remembers that after her father was fired from the government and party she wanted to storm the Munhumutapa offices to protest. She planned to arrive at the building in a T-shirt emblazoned with a picture of Mnangagwa and play the Jah Prayzah hit track 'Mdhara vachauya' (The old man will return). Her husband Gerald, however, dissuaded her.

'As a family at large, we didn't feel like we had to hide,' she says. 'We were, like, it's on, we are going to fight for our father, and if they want to kill every single one of us, they will have to do that. They are not touching our father, and whatever we can do to carry on with the struggle here, while he is there [South Africa], we will do it. We carried on with supporting the youth in Zanu-PF that supported him and doing whatever was necessary to keep his support alive. I also supported the ministers that had been behind Dad.'

Farai remembers sending a message to several embattled ministers who were facing expulsion from both the party and government because of their loyalty to Mnangagwa. A Politburo meeting held on 8 November had resolved to purge all his allies across the party's ten provinces, as well as firing him from the party. 'I sent a message to Chinamasa saying, Thank you that you have always stood by my Dad. He has always spoken very highly of you. The Mutsvangwas and several other people, I thought it was important to acknowledge them. I also sent to Oppah Muchinguri-Kashiri because they all knew that they were next. So we didn't shrink, we didn't coil, it was the complete opposite,' she says.

Her husband Gerald recalls the days that Mnangagwa was on the run as being an anxious time all round for the family. It was worsened by the fact that there were very few people who could be trusted.

Tarirai was at his home the night that Mnangagwa crossed into Mozambique. He was recounting to Gerald, Farai and her sisters their experience at the border post and the skirmishes with authorities.

'The most touching event he related was that of his uncle, Mnangagwa, telling the boys to go back home, as this was not their fight and that he didn't want them killed at all,' says Gerald. 'All of them refused to return to Harare, declaring that they would rather die making sure he crossed into Mozambique. There were tears all around the room, tears of relief, and tears of sisters empathising fully with their brothers and cousin risking all to ensure that their father would escape.'

When her father had safely crossed into Mozambique, a coded message was sent to Farai meant to inform the family of his safety. It read, 'The puzzle has been resolved.'

The purge of Mnangagwa's allies was to be a massive root-and-branch shake-up of the structures in Zanu-PF. But that the G40 faction had embarked on such a wide-scale expulsion of Lacoste members – whether they were senior government officials, parastatal heads, CEOs of private sector companies, or leaders of party provinces and districts – only showed the extent of Mnangagwa's support throughout the country.

10

A perfect plan

On the eve of Mnangagwa's dismissal by Mugabe, General Constantino Chiwenga travelled to China. He returned to Harare a week later on 12 November to find the country engulfed in a volatile political crisis. The highly inflammatory political atmosphere had been fuelled by the expulsion of Mnangagwa from government and party and his flight into exile. What Chiwenga would do or fail to do at that time was certain to have enormous consequences for the country.

A person interviewed for this book indicated that before the army general left for China, a meeting was held between Chiwenga, Mnangagwa and the war veterans' leader, Christopher Mutsvangwa, to discuss the events that had occurred in Bulawayo the previous day when Grace Mugabe was booed at White City Stadium. At that meeting on 5 November 2017, the source said, the decision was taken to deal with the deteriorating political situation.

On the same day, Grace Mugabe addressed what turned out to be her last rally at Rufaro Stadium. Her attacks on Mnangagwa were vicious and unrestrained and she likened Mnangagwa to a snake that had to have its head crushed.

A family member said Mnangagwa had followed the rally addressed by Grace, which was broadcast live on ZBC. His wife had come into the lounge and found her husband watching Grace insulting him, and switched off the TV. 'You will have high blood pressure,' she told him.

Instead, Mnangagwa got up and went to his car to listen to the speech on the radio. He had a notebook and pen in his hand and took notes of Grace's speech as she attacked him.

When Chiwenga returned from China and landed at Robert Gabriel Mugabe International Airport, an attempt was made by the police to arrest him on the instructions of the police commissioner, Augustine Chihuri. Chiwenga's trip was said by the Foreign Ministry to have been a normal 'military exchange mutually agreed upon by China and Zimbabwe'. Chiwenga met the Chinese defence minister, Chang Wanquan, in Beijing on 10 November. It seems this meeting was the reason why Mugabe ordered Chiwenga's arrest. According to the news agency Reuters, quoting two unnamed sources in a news report published on 26 November 2017, Chiwenga had asked his counterpart if China would agree not to interfere if he took temporary control in Zimbabwe so as to remove Mugabe from power. 'Chang assured him Beijing would not get involved and the two also discussed tactics that might be employed during the de facto coup,' the sources told Reuters. 'The pair [police commissioner Chihuri and his deputy Innocent Matibiri] assembled a squad of 100 police and intelligence agents. But the plot leaked and Chiwenga supporters managed to pull together a counter-team of several hundred Special Forces soldiers and agents as their commander's plane approached. Some were disguised as baggage handlers, their military fatigues and weapons hidden beneath high-visibility jackets and overalls, one security source said. Realising they were outnumbered and outgunned, Chihuri's police team backed down, allowing Chiwenga to touch down without incident, the security sources said.'

Reuters also reported that according to secret documents in its possession, Mugabe had summoned Chiwenga to attend a meeting in late October, whose purpose was to obtain Chiwenga's buy-in to support his wife Grace's accession to the presidency and to ditch Mnangagwa, with whom it was known Chiwenga had very close ties.

'Chiwenga was warned by Mugabe that it was high time for him to start supporting his wife. He mentioned to Chiwenga that those fighting her were bound to die a painful death. At the same meeting, Mugabe also ordered Chiwenga to pledge allegiance to Grace. He refused. Chiwenga refused to be intimidated. He stood his ground over his loyalty to Mnangagwa,' Reuters said, quoting a confidential intelligence report.

If there had been a concerted drive to create a rift between Mnangagwa and Chiwenga, what kind of relationship did the two men have? Was it one that was able to weather the storms of political life, I asked Farai.

'The relationship between Dad and Chiwenga is very close and they are like brothers. They have come a long way and I have witnessed it myself. They are very close,' she says.

Although the relationship was iron strong, there were anxious moments for Mnangagwa's family when both men were out of the country, Mnangagwa in exile in South Africa and Chiwenga in China. 'As a family we felt vulnerable because we thought Dad was vulnerable as Chiwenga was out of the country,' says Farai. 'We weren't sure if he [Chiwenga] had been sent out or he had deliberately gone out to avoid having to deal with this issue. A part of me wanted to believe that it's not possible for him to betray us; not the Chiwenga I know. I would convince myself over and over that they were working on something; no, they were working on something. They've got this, but my brothers were saying no. Emmerson Jnr in particular was saying, No, he has left us; he is not with us any more. And so I would get these negative reports, people saying that Chiwenga had deserted us.'

In those trying times of uncertainty and despondency, Farai turned to Mary Chiwenga, the general's wife, to find out what was happening. 'I would call Mary and say, What's going on? She was very evasive, but she would say, Farai, don't worry, he [your Dad] will be fine. I don't know what's going on either, but he will be fine. With hindsight now, I can see that she couldn't say anything, but whenever I spoke to her,

I didn't get the feeling that she was panicking and she didn't sound like somebody who had betrayed. So it gave me a little bit of confidence that something was being sorted out. What mattered was that Dad was out of the country. The Air Force also got hold of me, even after Dad was in South Africa, and they were like, Don't worry, we are behind your dad. By the time those statements started coming out that now we are going to step in and do this, then that made everything clear.'

When Chiwenga issued his statement on 13 November 2017, flanked by about a hundred senior army officers, Farai was elated. She said she knew at that point that it was 'game on' and understood exactly what Chiwenga's statement meant. 'When the war vets released their statement in South Africa and then Chiwenga also, for me it was confirmation that all was not lost. Then I knew that it was all coming together, and I was more confident now and was also ready to do whatever was necessary to help,' she says.

The appearance of Major-General Sibusiso Moyo on TV on 15 November was an emotional moment for Farai. She recalls crying 'like a baby'. For her it was the strongest confirmation that all would be well with her father and the nation.

Overjoyed by the sight of Moyo, who announced the army take-over, Farai went to see him so that she could personally express her gratitude. 'I gave him a hug and I told him that seeing him on TV was the best day of my life. This was really on our TV; something which you see on the movies when the army takes over the television studios and all. Moyo just smiled and did not say much.'

But had there ever been a perfect plan for Mugabe's removal or was it all mere luck?

Farai remonstrates. 'With hindsight, this thing was planned to the tee. I was so impressed. They are military guys. I think even when he was fired and we were at home that day and Dad was trying to figure out what he had to do, but he knew exactly what he was meant to do. His one mission was to get out of the country. If you noticed: he was out of the country, Chiwenga was out of the country, and Mutsvangwa was also out. There was a fourth person, somebody else very important, who was out. So Dad's mission was to just get out of the country. That's why I had those Air Force guys saying, We need to make sure that he has crossed the border. It was planned so well.'

That Mugabe fell from power was in part due to military planning whose finer details were hard to establish throughout the course of interviews for this book, but it was also aided by a combination of other factors. In the end, Mugabe had no friends in the region or abroad. The praise and admiration that he was long thought to evoke in the rest of the continent proved to be hollow. For after initially regarding what had happened in Zimbabwe as a coup, the African Union backtracked and soon welcomed the political transition headed by the military under Chiwenga.

At home, Mugabe had even fewer sympathisers. A wrecked economy, a worthless Zimbabwe dollar, foreign investor flight and the isolation of Zimbabwe from the international community were all he had to show for the last twenty years of his rule. Millions of Zimbabweans had been forced to leave the country for South Africa, Botswana, the UK, Canada and other countries.

'They [the military] read the mood perfectly,' Farai says. 'The timing as well was perfect, because with things like this, the timing is everything. The mood was ripe and everybody wanted Mugabe to go. If there is anything that united Zimbabweans, it was just that one fact that all of us wanted him gone, including the rest of the world. So even if it had been a military coup in the sense that it is defined conventionally, I don't think that the world would have condemned it. The world wanted Mugabe to go and I think they would have found a way to normalise the situation. Maybe they would have forced a unity government or something, but I don't think there is a single soul, except for Mugabe's wife, his kids and the G40, who wanted him to carry on.'

On 18 November, hundreds of thousands of citizens poured out onto the streets of Harare and sent a message to Mugabe that it was time to go. But would Mugabe, having vowed numerous times in the past that he would never step down, listen and leave without putting up a fight?

11

An emperor without clothes

According to a person with knowledge of the behind-the-scenes events, before the issuing of the military statement on 13 November 2017 General Constantino Chiwenga privately brought together the most senior army generals. 'Are you happy with what's going on? Because if we are going to do anything, we have to do this together and everybody needs to be on the same page,' Chiwenga is said to have told the generals.

'We are done with Mugabe. They cannot do this to Mnangagwa,' is the response that Chiwenga was given almost in unison, in what is said to have been a highly charged meeting. 'This man [Mnangagwa] is our commander.'

Hours later, Chiwenga issued his statement at KGVI Barracks (now renamed Josiah Magama Tongogara Barracks). Chiwenga's statement read:

It is with humility and a heavy heart that we come before you to pronounce the indisputable reality there is instability in Zanu-PF today and, as a result, anxiety in the country at large. Zimbabwe's history is hinged on the ideals of the revolution dating back to the First Chimurenga where thousands of people perished. Zanu-PF is the political party that waged the Second Chimurenga for our independence; the struggle in which many Zimbabweans, in one way or the other, sacrificed and contributed immensely to our liberation.

Many of these gallant fighters still live on with the spirited hope of seeing a prosperous Zimbabwe but also hope of leaving behind an inheritance and legacy for posterity. It is pertinent to restate that the Zimbabwe Defence Forces remain the major stakeholder and, when these are threatened, we are obliged to take corrective measures.

Clearly, Zanu-PF having in the main been the only party that has ruled this country since independence, it has become a household name to most Zimbabweans across the political divide. Therefore, it is common cause that any instability within the party naturally impacts on their social, political and economic lives. Accordingly, there is distress, trepidation and despondence within the nation. Our peace-loving people who have stood by their Government and endured some of the most trying social and economic conditions ever experienced are extremely disturbed by what is happening within the ranks of the national revolutionary party.

What is obtaining in the revolutionary party is a direct result of the machinations of counter-revolutionaries who have infiltrated the party and whose agenda is to destroy it from within. It is saddening to see our revolution being hijacked by agents of our erstwhile enemies who are now on the brink of returning our country to foreign domination against which so many of our people perished. The famous slogan espoused by His Excellency, the President of the Republic of Zimbabwe, Head of State and Government, and Commander-in-Chief of the Zimbabwe Defence Forces, Cde R.G. Mugabe – 'Zimbabwe will never be a colony again' – is being seriously challenged by counter-revolutionary infiltrators who are now effectively influencing the direction of the party. It is our strong and deeply considered position that if drastic action is not taken immediately, our beloved country Zimbabwe is definitely headed to becoming a neo-colony again.

The current purging and cleansing process in Zanu-PF, which

so far is targeting mostly members associated with liberation history, is a serious cause for concern to us in the Defence Forces. As a result of squabbling within the ranks of Zanu-PF, there has been no meaningful development in the country for the past five years. The resultant economic impasse has ushered in more challenges to the Zimbabwean populace, such as cash shortages and rising commodity prices.

Our revolutionary path is replete with conduct and rebellion by people who have attempted to destroy the revolution from within. The formation of FROLIZI, the attempt to remove the late Cde Herbert Chitepo from his position of chairman at the Mumbwa bogus congress in 1973, the Nhari-Badza rebellion, Ndabaningi Sithole's rebellion soon after the death of Cde Chitepo, the Vashandi 1 and 2 as well as the rebellion that led to the death of the late Zipra commander, Cde Alfred Nikita Mangena, among others, are cases in point.

Therefore, the current shenanigans by people who do not share the same liberation history of Zanu-PF are not surprises to us. But what is significant to us and the generality of Zimbabweans is to remember that all these rebellions were defused by the military, but at no point did the military usurp power. We must remind those behind the current treacherous shenanigans that when it comes to matters of protecting our revolution, the military will not hesitate to step in.

Zanu-PF's standing political virtues are a product of faithful adherence to the founding values, decorum, discipline and revolutionary protocol in the ruling party. Party orders were strictly adhered to and, whatever differences existed, they have been resolved amicably and in the ruling party's closet. Unfortunately, since the turn of 2015, Zanu-PF's traditional protocol and procedures have changed with a lot of gossiping, backbiting and public chastisement being the order of the day. Indeed, the party is undoing its legacy built over the years.

While our people may be persuaded to take what is going on in Zanu-PF as internal political matters in that party, the truth remains that Zanu-PF's conduct and behaviour as a ruling party has a direct impact on the lives of every citizen; hence all of us regardless of political affiliation are affected by the party's manner of doing business. From a security point of view we cannot ignore the experiences of countries, such as Somalia, DRC, Central Africa Republic and many others in our region, where minor political differences degenerated into serious conflict that has decimated the social, political and economic security of ordinary people.

Section 212 of the Constitution of Zimbabwe states that the aim of the Defence Forces is to protect Zimbabwe, its people, its national security and interests, and its territorial integrity, and to uphold this Constitution.

Among other security threats are the reckless utterances denigrating the military which are causing despondency within the rank and file. Further, we note with concern the attempts by some politicians to drive a wedge within the security services for their own selfish interests. This is unacceptable. We take great exception to this behaviour. There is only one Commander-in-Chief, His Excellency, the President, Head of State and Government, and Commander-in-Chief of the Zimbabwe Defence Forces, Cde. R.G. Mugabe.

The military is an institution whose roles cut across the wider spectrum of government support functions in the form of military aid to civil power and military aid to civil ministries, which are roles derived from defence instruments. Therefore we want to state here and now that the history of our revolution cannot be rewritten by those who have not been part of it. Having said that, we strongly urge the Party:

- To stop reckless utterances by politicians from the ruling party denigrating the military, which is causing alarm and despondency within the rank and file.

- The current purging, which is clearly targeting members of the party with a liberation background, must stop.
- The known counter-revolutionary elements who have fomented the current instability in the party must be exposed and fished out.
- As the party goes for the Extraordinary Congress, members must go with an equal opportunity to exercise their democratic rights.

Comrades and friends, ladies and gentlemen, we remain committed to protecting our legacy, and those bent on hijacking the revolution will not be allowed to do so. Further, we must understand that the freedoms that we enjoy today were as a result of supreme sacrifice by some of our countrymen and women, and this must not be taken for granted. Let us remove this air of uncertainty and allow Zimbabweans to enjoy their freedoms and rights as enshrined in the national Constitution.

If the account of the meeting among the generals prior to Chiwenga's public announcement is indeed true, then the decision by the military to side with Mnangagwa was driven by an allegiance to a person they viewed as one of their own. There is an unwritten principle that permeates the military in Zimbabwe: that once a soldier, always a soldier. For the military generals, Mnangagwa was one of their own. A former guerrilla fighter, he had trained in Egypt and China and was also the head of military intelligence in Mozambique in the late 1970s. The generals had a long history of association with Mnangagwa that stretched back to the front lines of the liberation struggle against the Rhodesian government. Mnangagwa was also the defence minister from 2009 until 2013, during the five-year term of the Government of National Unity. Even though Mnangagwa left the army barracks for political office, all indications are that his ties with the military remained intact and ran deep.

That the generals 'were done with Mugabe' suggests that their allegiance had shifted. Mugabe had lost control of the army, though he still held the title of commander-in-chief. But when exactly did power move away from him? It seems that the erosion of the military's loyalty took place over a period of time. Instead of an overnight change of heart, there was a slow build-up of tensions until they reached boiling point. This came when Mnangagwa was fired. His dismissal had the effect of exposing the shift in power that had happened under Mugabe's watch. The emperor was left without clothes.

That a covert 'vote of no confidence' was passed on Mugabe in the corridors of the army barracks firstly before a motion of impeachment against him came in Parliament a week later is most significant. The generals, it is clear, were never prepared to entertain a 'plea bargain' from Mugabe, which would buy him more time at the helm of the country. More importantly, the military's vote of no confidence confirms that there can be no Zimbabwean leader who does not have the full support of the military; and it also shows how interwoven the military and politics are in Zimbabwe. The claim that 'politics always leads the gun', as was often said by Mugabe in a bid to contain his restless military generals, did not turn out to be true.

Since the turn of the new millennium there had already been several instances when the military generals sent out a gentle reminder to the rest of the nation of their kingmaking status. On 9 January 2002, the late army commander Vitalis Zvinavashe, flanked by other top generals, said in a statement that the military would never salute a leader without liberation credentials. The pointed reference was to Morgan Tsvangirai, whose newly formed Movement for Democratic Change had emerged as the first political party to pose a real challenge to Zanu-PF's rule since independence in 1980. In 2011, Brigadier-General Douglas Nyikayaramba also sent out another reminder to the MDC of the military's role-making power, ahead of the 2013 elections.

But the statement of 13 November 2017 issued by Chiwenga was not a gentle reminder meant for outsiders. It was the reading of the riot act to a political organisation, Zanu-PF, a public assertion that the military also had a vested interest in the politics of the country. The tables had turned on Mugabe, Zanu-PF's leader.

* * *

A central role in laying the groundwork for the eventual fall of Mugabe from power was played by the war veterans. One of the ways in which this happened was by calling into question Mugabe's liberation credentials. Having spent years expertly stitching together a narrative of being a great African liberator and neocolonial fighter against the West, Mugabe could ill afford any tarnishing of his reputation. Central to the unstitching of Mugabe's liberation credentials was Christopher Mutsvangwa, the war veterans' leader and a staunch ally of Mnangagwa. He reminded his audiences that Mugabe had never achieved the leadership of the ruling party owing to any significant military exploit but had been invited to join the liberation struggle in Mozambique. In Mutsvangwa's account, far from being a fighter, Mugabe was cast merely as an eloquent orator, assigned to speak on behalf of Zanu-PF at a time when it lacked articulate spokespeople.

But it was not only Mutsvangwa who shone a spotlight on Mugabe's contribution to the liberation struggle. Members of Mugabe's own inner circle also lifted the mask that covered Africa's last remaining liberator-president. In an interview with Heidi Holland, Jonathan Moyo, who had a love–hate relationship with Mugabe over the years, said: 'Looking at the record, he comes home on holiday; a man bringing his future wife to meet his family and intending to return to Ghana as a teacher to teach. He wants to settle in Ghana, where he has a well-paid job, which he hasn't resigned from. And then the Rhodesian nationalist movement, which is going through turbulence including leadership turbulence, hears of him, this articulate man called Robert Mugabe. Word goes around that he trains teachers so he is more articulate than the teachers, who are the most respected people in the country at that time. And of all exciting places, he lives and works in Ghana, where Nkrumah is leading the way to African liberation. He has Fort Hare qualifications. His wife is impressive. So he is approached, persuaded to join the liberation movement, and he agrees to give it a try.

'Nowhere in his record prior to becoming leader of Zanu do you see Robert Mugabe driven by political passion or a vision of a better future for Zimbabweans. He has not left his well-paid job in Ghana to join the nationalist movement at home. No, not at all. He has simply taken leave to go on a visit to Rhodesia. Nowhere is there any logical progression from there to the Marxism he espouses so eloquently later on. The man who comes from Ghana in the early 1960s is not a Marxist.'

Being an eloquent speaker, well dressed and acquainted with British manners, Mugabe was approached by the armed wing of Zanu-PF, the Zimbabwe National Liberation Army, to be its face in the peace negotiations with Britain at the Lancaster House talks. His smoothness, eloquence and polished demeanour, the military generals opined, would be a much better proposition at the negotiating table with the British than rugged and uncouth combatants.

So when it came in late 2017 for the military to choose between Mnangagwa and Mugabe, the generals saw a reflection of themselves in Mnangagwa, a fellow decorated fighter, whereas in Mugabe they saw only a political leader, a mouthpiece, whose stay in power depended on their say-so.

When a long-term view is taken of the breakdown in relations between Mugabe and the military, a decisive moment can be seen to have occurred in July 2016. Then the war veterans' association, an affiliate of the military, announced that they had decided to cut ties with Mugabe, saying that supporting him in the 2018 elections was suicidal. This decision to dump Mugabe had been sparked by the wave of confrontations and attacks that the war veterans had suffered at the hands of Grace Mugabe and the G40 faction. 'We, the veterans of Zimbabwe's war of liberation, together with our toiling masses, hereby declare that henceforth, in any forthcoming elections, we will not support such a leader who has presided over untold suffering of the general population for his own personal aggrandizement and that of his cronies.'

In an analysis published in the *Mail & Guardian*, the peace and security researcher Gwinyai Dzinesa said that Mugabe's end was inevitable the moment the war veterans cut ties with him in 2016. 'Mugabe's dictatorial leadership, and his failure to stop Zimbabwe's economic meltdown, corruption, widespread poverty, and the ascendancy of the G40 amid expelling of liberation war stalwarts, deepened the Zimbabwe National Liberation War Veterans Association (ZNLWVA) grievances. In November 2016, the influential ZNLWVA scrapped the position of patron, which Mugabe held, from their constitution. This sealed the ZNLWVA's divorce from Mugabe, whom they dubbed "a hard-sell" for Zanu-PF in Zimbabwe's 2018 national elections. The writing was on the wall for Mugabe.'

After the parting of ways between Mugabe and the war veterans, who were once his most ardent defenders and who had led the farm invasions in 2000, Mugabe surrounded himself with new foot soldiers. It was the Zanu-PF Youth League, an arm of the G40 faction, that filled the void left by the war veterans. They became Mugabe's new defenders and praise singers. Alongside Grace Mugabe, the Zanu-PF Youth League became involved in a frontal assault against the war veterans and the military.

The brazen attacks by Grace on the military incensed the generals, who were further angered by Mugabe's apparent reluctance to restrain his wife. Was she the proxy through which he was indirectly attacking them? Mugabe always appeared to be in her corner, even when she charged that the military was plotting to kill her children.

In the midst of the brewing tensions, Mugabe would often remind his listeners that politics led the gun and not the other way round. This was said in an attempt to project himself as being still fully in charge. In

July 2017, Mugabe told a meeting of the Zanu-PF Women's League in Harare that he was aware that some top commanders in the military were agitating for his removal from office. 'There are secret manoeuvres going on. The military has no right to be interfering with the political processes. Theirs is to support; they can give their own views within the constitution and according, also, to the principle that politics shall always lead the gun – and not the gun leading politics. That would be a coup. Look at what is happening: top commanders are saying the President must now leave office. They want me to leave? Who is going to take my place? Who is their preferred leader? It's disgraceful for anyone to say, "I am the one now in charge, the president must go." Beating your own chest and declaring that, yes, you're the one taking over? No, we don't want that. We don't want that.'

In addition, Mugabe's silence in the face of Grace's unrelenting attacks also emboldened her G40 faction to belittle and humiliate the military. The same tactic of striking hard that had been used by Grace and the G40 to decimate the Joice Mujuru faction in Zanu-PF was now turned against any person or institution viewed as a stumbling block to her rise to the presidency. Not only did Grace publicly attack the military several times, but her closest ally, Jonathan Moyo, was vocal in criticism of General Chiwenga. Moyo questioned Chiwenga's academic qualifications and also belittled the command agriculture programme, meant to promote food self-sufficiency in Zimbabwe, which had the support of the military.

As Zimbabwe slipped into crisis after the Chiwenga statement of 13 November, the G40 faction continued on its warpath against the military. On that day, Kudzai Chipanga, the Zanu-PF Youth League chairperson, was sent to carry out a hatchet job on behalf of the faction. Chipanga addressed a press conference at the Zanu-PF headquarters in response to the military statement, where he said that the views expressed by Chiwenga were his 'personal opinion' and did not represent the 'collective view' of the entire top brass.

Either it was plain naivety on the part of the G40 faction that caused it to fail to notice the winds of change blowing, or it was still caught up in the false sense of invincibility that had become its prominent feature. This invincibility was supremely expressed by Grace, who derided all her political rivals, without regard for the consequences, though she herself had only just recently entered active politics.

Soon after Chipanga's press briefing, information minister Simon Khaya-Moyo responded to Chiwenga's statement with a false sense of bravado. He said that Chiwenga's message to the ruling party reeked of treason. Khaya-Moyo's statement read:

Consistent with the guiding principle of the national liberation struggle, the ruling Zimbabwe African National Union Patriotic Front (Zanu-PF) reaffirms the primacy of politics over the gun. It is against an understanding of this abiding principle that the statement issued by General Constantino Chiwenga purporting to speak on behalf of the Zimbabwe Defence Forces (ZDF) was not only surprising, but was an outrageous vitiation of professional soldiership and his wartime record as a high-ranking freedom fighter entrusted with command responsibilities in a free democratic Zimbabwe. Clearly calculated to disturb national peace and stability, the said statement by General Constantino Chiwenga, which was not signed, and which did not represent the rest of the command element, suggests treasonable conduct on his part as this was meant to incite insurrection and violent challenge to the constitutional order. Indeed, this is what happens when the gun seeks to overreach by dictating to politics and norms of constitutionality. As the party running the democratically elected Government of Zimbabwe, Zanu-PF will never succumb to any threats, least of all those deriving from conduct that is inconsistent with the tenets of democracy and constitutionalism. Not too far back, the President and First Secretary of Zanu-PF, Cde R.G. Mugabe, who is also Commander-in-Chief of the Zimbabwe Defence Forces, reminded members of the uniformed forces of their subordinate place and role vis-à-vis the political authority of the land. By yesterday's reprehensible conduct, it would appear that this wise counsel not only went unheeded but was flagrantly flouted in deference to factional politics and personal ambitions. Such conduct stands unreservedly condemned not only in the party but also in our Southern African region and the entire African continent, where subversion of constitutional authority is frowned upon and regarded as an absolute anathema.

Whatever might happen next, all sides had made their choices. There was no going back. Whoever blinked first would blink their last.

12

Mugabe's last supper

With hearty chuckles to diffuse the tension, raised voices, arguing and a repeated back and forth: that is how former president Robert Mugabe and his wife, Grace, reflected on the events that led to their ousting from power, four months after the army tanks rolled into Harare on the night of 14 November 2017. Their removal from power has come and gone, but the memory of the event is still fresh. They have forgotten little. On 15 March 2018 the once all-powerful couple opened up their palatial home in Borrowdale, dubbed the 'Blue Roof', to a select number of foreign and local journalists including the London *Times*, the South African Broadcasting Corporation and ITV News. It was an attempt by the couple to tell their side of the story.

In essence, Mugabe feels betrayed: by Emmerson Mnangagwa, his former vice-president; by Constantino Chiwenga, his former army commander; and by the ruling party, Zanu-PF. As for Mnangagwa, Mugabe insists he is 'illegal and illegitimate where he is'. At the same time, he refers to Mnangagwa as a 'son' and, although he falls short of calling him disobedient, he likens him to a son who does not always listen to his father. 'I don't hate Mnangagwa and I want to work with him. But he must be proper to be where he is. He is illegal. We must undo this disgrace we have imposed on ourselves. We don't deserve it.

Zimbabwe does not deserve it. We want to be a constitutional country. We must obey the law,' Mugabe says.

But while Mugabe points fingers, the betrayal that he speaks of masks another feeling: one of disappointment. His political end is one which neither he nor Grace had envisaged. The circumstances of their departure make their pain of being forced out even greater – despite the attempt by Mugabe to project himself as a willing participant in events, ready to step down to prevent 'bloodshed'.

Mugabe had seen and been through it all. In his thirty-seven years in office, he had observed seven US presidents: Jimmy Carter, Ronald Reagan, George H.W. Bush, Bill Clinton, George W. Bush, Barack Obama and Donald Trump. He was the ultimate survivor, lasting through a period of severe economic meltdown in which Zimbabwe achieved the world's highest rate of hyper-inflation and experienced two decades of Western sanctions. With such feats under his belt, for the self-proclaimed 'Lion of Africa' to leave by resigning was both shameful and disappointing.

'We didn't exactly know what was happening,' Grace said of the events of November 2017. The admission that the Mugabes never saw the military action coming their way is surprising. It either confirms the military precision of 'Operation Restore Legacy' or exposes the false sense of security that had gripped Mugabe and members of his inner circle. Even when she first saw a video clip on her cellphone of Chiwenga making his announcement, Grace says she did not believe it. 'Someone had sent me that information on my phone. I replied, I don't think it's true that Chiwenga made this statement.'

She only believed the truth of it after she asked 'Baba' (Father), as she calls Mugabe, on Tuesday night. Mugabe had come home after holding a cabinet meeting. 'When I found Baba here on Tuesday, I asked him and he said, Yes, you can look at the dressing table, there is a statement that was made by Chiwenga. I then read it and I said, Oh, so it's true. Then we went down to eat, but things were just starting, tanks were moving from Inkomo Barracks into the city. We were not

sure what exactly was happening. We ate, then went up [to the lounge],'
Grace says.

But what were Mugabe's thoughts of the statement by his army
general? Surely he should have been alarmed? 'I thought he [Chiwenga]
would have at least informed me and listed all the problems and
informed me of the dissatisfaction which they have,' Mugabe says.
That he had expected his army commander to speak to him directly
perhaps explains the rather curious response given to Chiwenga's
statement by Simon Khaya-Moyo, the party spokesperson who also
doubled up as the information minister. By sending Khaya-Moyo to
respond to Chiwenga, Mugabe was intent on putting on a brave face.
Ignoring the general and instead sending a party spokesperson was
also meant to put Chiwenga in his place, to touch his ego.

While Mugabe tried by all means to project an aura of normality
in the conduct of government business, it would not take long before
the pretensions of being in control fell away. The centre was no longer
holding.

In their palatial home, the Mugabes were cut off from the unfolding events on the ground. This isolation from reality seems to have
taken hold in all kinds of ways. While the military tanks were making their way into the city, Mugabe and his ministers were gathered
together in a cabinet meeting but had switched off their phones and
so were oblivious of the activity outside. It turned out to be the last
full cabinet meeting that Mugabe ever chaired. 'I don't think even the
cabinet ministers knew, it was just between himself [Chiwenga] and a
few of them that knew,' Grace adds.

Mugabe chips in that he tried to find out about the tank movements. 'The tanks are only three, we don't have more and these I
think were gifts. I was told that the tanks were going to another destination: Mutare, Manicaland, somewhere. They are ancient ones, very
ancient. They were as ancient as uMzilikazi. They had never been
used anywhere and nobody is using tanks any more nowadays; they
use armoured cars, which are faster.'

The couple break out into laughter, amused by Mugabe's insistence that the country has only three military tanks – though these were enough to topple him from power.

Insulated from the events that were taking place outside, the couple only awoke to the seriousness of the situation when the finance minister, Ignatius Chombo, raised the alarm. He called the Mugabes to inform them that there was a 'tense situation out there'. But as there was little that they could do, the Mugabes prepared to go to sleep.

'But at about 11 p.m. or going on midnight, Baba got a call from [the police commissioner] Augustine Chihuri saying that the soldiers are at ZBC [Zimbabwe Broadcasting Corporation] and they have taken over and they are already making a statement,' Grace says.

Three hours later, Chihuri called Mugabe again, to break the news that 'this is a real coup, there is a coup already taking place in Zimbabwe'. It was to be the start of a long night for the Mugabes.

Grace recalls that at the same time, a distress call came through to her from two allies and ministers, Jonathan Moyo and Saviour Kasukuwere. 'Literally Jonathan was crying, Mama, help us, we are going to be killed. I could hear the sound of guns in the background, because they were shooting at the house, attacking them. That's the time I decided that I had to rescue them. I started crying, because the sound was quite bad of the shooting. Then I said to Baba, They are going to kill them, what do we do?'

Two vehicles with security personnel from Blue Roof were dispatched to Kasukuwere's house in Helensvale. They were asked to bring Kasukuwere and Moyo with their families to the Mugabe home.

'When they [the security team] got there, they [the soldiers] saw cars coming, the soldiers who were attacking ran away,' says Grace. 'We were told there were about 40 soldiers who were attacking the place. Fortunately for the families who were in the house, the bullets could not penetrate the glass because that glass is tempered. When they got there, the gate had been sort of bombed, so I hear. But then Kasukuwere was afraid to go to the gate, but I urged him on, I said, I will keep the phone open until the security get to your house. Then they managed to rescue Kasukuwere, the rest of the families. They came here and it was about 4 a.m. in the morning.'

Mugabe agreed that the families of Kasukuwere and Moyo could shelter at his property. However, he asked the two men to leave and find their own place to stay. But before they left, Grace says they all sat together for about an hour. The Mugabes, Moyo and Kasukuwere were 'shocked', she said, by the events that had unfolded.

'We just sat and we talked probably for an hour or so, but we said, You can't stay here. We asked them to go. But Baba said, Let's keep the mothers and children on humanitarian grounds. I received them and we went to sit. It was like a situation where you don't talk much, because we were in shock, all of us. Baba and I, we are not really people who are impulsive such that when you hear something, then you react.'

Contrary to rumours that the Mugabes escaped to the Far East or that Grace went to Namibia, the couple remained indoors at their home. It was the start of a long waiting game. They waited for some sort of indication from the military of what would happen next. But there were no new developments.

From the Mugabes' version of events, it appears that although the military broadcast had given an assurance to the nation that the president and his family were 'safe and sound', there had not yet been any contact between the Mugabes and the generals.

Meanwhile, the soldiers and police who guarded their property continued to do so. Neither army tanks nor soldiers came into the grounds of the sprawling forty-four-acre mansion during that time.

'We didn't know what to do,' says Grace. 'We could not call any-body, we were here, but later on my siblings and my relatives started coming, to enquire about what had transpired. We just sat in the house, we remained in here, and after a day or two, because we were just seated, we were just going to sleep and talking with Kasukuwere's and Moyo's families.'

One night as they sat up in their lounge, Grace said the couple decided to ask for help 'in the interests of peace and stability for the country'. 'We looked around and said, Why don't we call Gideon Gono? And we did that. We didn't have anyone to send to Chiwenga. He came and then Baba talked to him and said, We have been here and we have been discussing issues and probably now is the third day and we don't know what's going to happen. Please go and tell Chiwenga that if it's power that he wants, we can give him.'

Gono is a former governor of the Reserve Bank of Zimbabwe and former chief executive officer of CBZ bank, the country's largest bank by depositors. He is also rumoured to have been close to Grace Mugabe.

At about 11 p.m., Gono was dispatched by the Mugabes to approach Chiwenga with the message 'If it's power that you want, we can hand over to him' because in the 'interests of peace we don't want bloodshed'.

Three hours later, Gono called Mugabe and reported back about the meeting he had managed to hold with the army commander.

Grace says that at 'some point' Mugabe had also managed to call Chiwenga on his mobile phone and got through to him. 'He continued to answer our calls. And then we said to him, But we sent a message to you that you can take over power if that's what you want. He said, No no no, that's not what we want, Baba should not think like so; that's not it. He refused. So then we said, What is it that they want? There is this impasse, how do we go about resolving it?'

13

The negotiating table

Robert Mugabe is an astute negotiator, a quality built up over the thirty-seven years when he was at the helm in Zimbabwe. In almost every decade of his rule, there was an event that required him to take a seat at the negotiating table. The outcomes, more often than not, were in his favour.

In 1979, Mugabe was part of the group of Zimbabwean nationalists who attended the Lancaster House talks and negotiated a peace deal with Britain, the former colonial master. As a result of their efforts, Zimbabwe was born the following year, in April 1980. After independence, Mugabe served as prime minister for seven years from 1980 until 1987, when he became president. In that first year of Mugabe's presidential rule, he faced his first major test. In the mid-1980s thousands of civilians in the Matabeleland and Midlands regions of the country had been murdered in what became known as the 'Gukurahundi' killings, which were carried out by the North Korean–trained 5th Brigade of the Zimbabwean army. When the atrocities could no longer be swept under the carpet and with international pressure mounting, Mugabe had to sit at the negotiation table with his major political opponent of the time, Joshua Nkomo, whose Ndebele people had been the target of the killings. A peace deal was struck and a unity accord was signed on 22 December 1987, which saw the union of Nkomo's Zapu party with Zanu. Critics of the accord believed the agreement benefited Mugabe the most.

About a decade later, Zimbabwe was faced with the most serious economic crisis since independence as rising prices and runaway inflation began to take their toll on the livelihoods of the country's citizens. At the same time, the veterans of the independence war demanded compensation for their contribution to the liberation struggle. Pushed into a corner, Mugabe went to the negotiation table to strike a deal with the war veterans. The latter got what they wanted and Mugabe received a stay of execution in respect of his political life. However, the biggest loser was the economy. The nadir of the economic meltdown was 'Black Friday', 14 November 1997, when the Zimbabwe dollar crashed and lost more than 70 per cent of its value against the US dollar. It became clear that the payouts to the veterans had overwhelmed the fiscus.

In September 2008 Mugabe was once again at the negotiation table, in a bid to salvage his political career after a new party, the Movement for Democratic Change, first formed in 1999 on the back of trade unions and student activists, secured a lead in the general elections of that year. The announcement of the election results was, however, delayed by a month. And when they were finally disclosed, it turned out that none of the contenders, Mugabe or Morgan Tsvangirai, had managed to clinch an outright win. The second round of voting was marred by violence orchestrated by the military to ensure Mugabe's victory. Tsvangirai then pulled out of the contest and vowed that he would not 'walk into State House over the dead bodies of Zimbabweans'. A political crisis erupted. Regional leaders from SADC, led by South African president Thabo Mbeki, stepped in and helped broker a peace deal. With his back against the wall, Mugabe was forced to the negotiation table and made to share power with Tsvangirai in a Government of National Unity.

Yet again, the outcome of the agreement largely favoured Mugabe. Although he had lost the first round of voting, he secured control of all the key portfolios in government such as defence and security. The service ministries, such as health and education, were given to Tsvangirai. Clearly, Mugabe wanted to offload onto Tsvangirai the unenviable task of cleaning up the economic mess he had created.

* * *

In November 2017 Mugabe returned again to the negotiation table to secure a political lifeline. This time, the odds were heavily stacked against him. He was isolated from his wartime comrades, he had no friends abroad and his own party had disowned him. Zimbabwe's economy was in shambles and millions of Zimbabweans had scattered abroad seeking refuge from the economic meltdown.

What drove Mugabe to reach out to the military? Is it that he genuinely believed he could be given a last chance or had he read the writing on the wall and decided to leave as much as possible on his own terms?

The Mugabes' plotting in the Blue Roof mansion suggests that legacy issues may have loomed large, although this was not what they gave as their motive for reaching out to the military through their proxy, Gideon Gono. After initially spurning Mugabe's attempts to 'discuss' matters, as he put it, the generals played ball and dispatched their own negotiators. It was the start of a series of marathon meetings held at Blue Roof and State House over nearly a week.

On 16 November Father Fidelis Mukonori and George Charamba arrived to negotiate on behalf of the military. Father Mukonori is a Jesuit priest and long-time confidant of Mugabe, while Charamba was Mugabe's spokesperson and permanent secretary at the Ministry of Information. Mugabe's emissary, Gono, joined the negotiations, and later so did Aaron Nhepera, the CIO director.

The discussions initially seem to have always started with Robert Mugabe, and only at his request would Grace Mugabe join in. It is not clear whether she deliberately avoided being part of the negotiation process or whether she was waiting for her husband's invitation.

The first issue brought to the couple's attention by Mukonori and Charamba was the statement presented by Kudzai Chipanga, the Youth League leader, on 14 November denigrating the military generals. They claimed it had been written by Grace herself. In an interview with the Johannesburg *Sunday Times*, published on 18 March 2018, Grace Mugabe denied this as being ridiculous.

'I said, What? What are you saying? Are you saying I wrote the statement for him? In fact I have been very busy and I don't even know where Chipanga lives. I don't communicate with Chipanga that much. Yes, we work together in the party, but I am not in the habit of doing those things.'

The core issues that were brought to Mugabe's attention in a written document that the negotiators brought with them from the military included the following:

- The politicians had to stop their 'reckless utterances' against the military, which were causing alarm and despondency among the ordinary people.
- Zanu-PF had to afford every party member a fair and equal chance of being heard or elected, democratic procedures had to be observed at all levels within the party, and candidates were no longer to be imposed on the party.
- All purges in the party and government were to cease and all previous victims of such purges were to be reinstated.
- The recommendations of the War Veterans' Indaba were to be implemented, and all war veterans were to be reintegrated into the mainstream of the party and government.
- Known 'counter-revolutionary elements' who had fomented the current instability in the party were to be removed.
- Security of employment, as provided for in the Constitution of Zimbabwe, was to be guaranteed.

On hearing the issues that the negotiators wished to discuss, Grace Mugabe thought Father Mukonori and Charamba were 'a bit biased'.

'Naturally they feared the army. So they were talking about restoring the legacy of the president and dealing with the so-called criminals around him. But they never mentioned my name in that document [of issues], I wasn't mentioned.'

On 17 November, the eve of the nationwide demonstrations that had been called for by the war veterans, Father Mukonori and Charamba went to Blue Roof once again to continue negotiations after Mugabe had returned from a graduation ceremony. As seems to have been the practice, Mugabe initially spoke to them alone but later called for Grace to come and join them. She recalls in her *Sunday Times* interview: 'When I got there I found him [Mugabe] on the phone talking. He told me that he was talking to ED [Mnangagwa]. They had just handed him over the phone by Father Mukonori. Where are you? he said to Mnangagwa, who replied, I am in South Africa. Baba asked him, Why did you leave? I think that is where Mnangagwa refers to Baba as having forgotten that he had fired him, but it's not true. Baba knew that he had actually fired Mnangagwa. Baba was just saying, But why did you leave [the country]. He then started explaining to him that some people wanted to strangle him with a string, so he was told by his own security that he had to leave the country because his life was in danger. So he had left.

'Baba said then, OK, you come back, we talk. We cannot discuss anything while you are there. I was listening and he [Mnangagwa] said, If you want me to come back, I will come back. I think that at that point Father Mukonori was very happy that he [Mnangagwa] had decided to come back so that they could go to the negotiating table to talk about these issues.'

Having secured an agreement that Mnangagwa would return from South Africa and meet Mugabe to iron out their differences, Grace said they were surprised by the turn of events the next day. 'But then the following day on Saturday, they organised demonstrations. We saw people at the stadium demonstrating, all saying that Mugabe must go.'

Hundreds of thousands of people had turned up on the streets of Harare. But the Mugabes made light of the turnout and were largely unmoved. Grace watched the street demonstrations on TV with her sister and the families of Moyo and Kasukuwere who were sheltering at their home. Like her husband, Grace belittled the demonstrations and seems to have followed them for amusement.

With the political temperature rising rapidly, the number of visitors making their way to Blue Roof increased. Top government figures such as Misheck Sibanda, the chief secretary of the cabinet; Happyton Bonyongwe, the justice minister; and Prince Machaya, the Attorney General, joined Father Mukonori and Charamba. Grace, who sat in on the negotiations, said the group mostly wanted to talk about what was happening outside: the street demonstrations and the start of the impeachment process in Parliament.

Mugabe insisted that there were no grounds for him to be pressured into stepping down. His reluctance stemmed from the conversation he had had with Mnangagwa, where a gentleman's agreement had been reached that his former deputy would first return and then they would start proper negotiations. Mugabe was in fact defiant. He refused to step down, despite the pressure being brought to bear on him by his senior government officials. 'They can go ahead,' Mugabe is said to have shot back when told about the plan to impeach him.

If Grace's account is anything to go by, she emerges as the uncelebrated heroine who got her husband to resign from office. She claims that it was she who reminded her husband of the agreement they had made in the aftermath of the military intervention that they were prepared to hand over power. 'He was very much ebbed by the fact that people wanted to impeach him, so he said they can go ahead. I said, Baba, it's not necessary, it takes a long time to do the impeachment process and it's not something they can do overnight. You know how sometimes he is strong, he said, Let them go ahead. Then I said, Please, please, just put pen to paper. If I wasn't there, he wasn't going to do it, because I said, Just do it. If it was just the man alone, he was not going to do it. But I said, Baba, just put pen to paper and just give it to them. So he did that.'

Her statements are revealing. She claims to have been able to convince her husband to stand down. This suggests that she had the greatest influence on Mugabe in the sunset years of his rule. Yet if she did wield so much direct power, why had she never been able to convince him previously to step down and name a successor, as she once asked him to do at a Zanu-PF Women's League meeting? Did the power and influence that Grace had over Mugabe also have its limits?

Despite her own growing political power and the widespread perception that Mugabe was grooming her to take over from him, Grace denies that she had any ambitions to become president. In fact she says it is 'nonsensical' to state that she had ever wanted to succeed her husband. Had it not been for the military action, her plan had been to reject the growing calls from the party's provinces and the Youth and Women's Leagues for her to become the next vice-president. Instead, she claims that she wanted the minister of defence, Sydney Sekeramayi, to take over from her husband. Her stance, in part, seems to have been informed by the view that Jonathan Moyo had expressed that Sekeramayi was more senior to Mnangagwa and was a more qualified alternative. 'I think I would have gone for him [Sekeramayi], to tell the truth. I don't mince my words. I know Sekeramayi is not a cruel person. I know Sekeramayi would not have taken the retribution as far as it has been taken, because a lot of people are suffering. I have lived with Mugabe for thirty years, he is a seasoned politician. Yes, they are denigrating him today, but he is one person that is very accommodative. Even if he hears that they are saying negative things against him, he wouldn't ask. That's what we call magnanimity, leadership qualities.'

After the telephone conversation with Mnangagwa, Mugabe's plan was that the two would attend the party congress where a democratic process of election for the leadership would be followed. Whoever emerged victorious would take over the reins of the party. When

Mugabe appeared on the state broadcaster on 19 November, a day after the protests, these were the sentiments he expressed in what was his last televised speech.

But his plan never materialised. Mugabe genuinely believed that he had popular support and could have defeated Mnangagwa at congress. But things never came to this point.

In her interview, Grace admitted that going to congress was their idea, after her husband's phone conversation with Mnangagwa. 'What surprised us was that Baba had managed to talk to Mnangagwa to say, Come, let's talk. The idea he had was, Come and let's go to congress. If the people are going to elect you, it's fine, but I think he [Mnangagwa] avoided that process because he knew that he was not going to win.

'He then made a statement that he was not going to come. Instead he was saying, You [Mugabe] said if the people speak that you must go, you will go. But only those MDC people in Harare? But it's not everyone, because if you go to the rural areas today, they are still questioning why Mugabe is no longer the president of this country. They say, We know Mugabe to be the president and we were preparing for the elections and to go with Mugabe as our candidate. Where is Mugabe? The people want answers. Things were not done in the proper manner.'

* * *

Mnangagwa's own version of what happened is somewhat different. He made a statement in response to the Mugabes' claims, saying:

My attention has been drawn to the press statement issued by the Commander of the Zimbabwe Defence Forces, General Constantino Guveya Chiwenga. I can confirm that President Robert Gabriel Mugabe made contact with me and invited me to return home for a discussion on the current political events in the nation. I told the President that I would not return home now until I am satisfied of my personal security, because of the manner and treatment given to me upon being fired. Given the events that followed my dismissal on Monday, 6th November 2017, at 4.00 p.m., my security details assigned to me and at my residency were immediately withdrawn. This was contrary to all the protocols that have existed in Zimbabwe to former State Vice-Presidents of the Republic of Zimbabwe. Security personnel, who are friendly to me, warned me that plans were underway to eliminate me once arrested and taken to a police station. It was in my security interest to leave the country immediately.

In my contact with President Mugabe I told the President that the current political and constitutional crisis in the country is not a matter between him and myself but between the people of Zimbabwe and President Mugabe. The people of Zimbabwe have clearly spoken on this matter.

To me the voice of the people is the voice of God, and their lack of trust and confidence in the leadership of President Mugabe has been expressed. Several groups, including students, general workers, opposition party members, vendors, religious organizations and ordinary citizens led by our war veterans, our party members in Zanu-PF, civic society, and all races of colour and creed in Zimbabwe, clearly demonstrated without violence their insatiable desire to have the resignation of His Excellency, Cde Robert Gabriel Mugabe. This was done on the following dates:

- The mass solidarity demonstrations led by the War Veterans on Saturday, 18th November 2017;
- The fully legally constituted Special Session of the CC [Central Committee of Zanu-PF] culminating in resolutions which were taken by the Session on Sunday, 19th November 2017;
- And the resolution by the Zanu-PF Parliamentary Caucus on Monday, 20th November 2017, to institute impeachment proceedings against the President, are all testimony that the President has lost the trust and confidence of the people of Zimbabwe.

The people of Zimbabwe have spoken with one voice and it is my appeal to President Mugabe that he should take heed of this clarion call by the people of Zimbabwe to resign so that the country can move forward and preserve his legacy. The ZDF Intervention through the Motto codenamed 'Operation Restore Legacy' is aimed at preserving the ethos of our struggle against British Colonialism, which was led by the late Dr J.M.N. Nkomo, Cde Robert Mugabe and many others. This fight included a struggle for social and economic empowerment which is all but lost now due to reasons clearly stated in the Impeachment Call by Zanu-PF Members of Parliament. The legacy of our struggle to unite the land with the people and the people with their land, championed by our war veterans and our people, defended by the gallant fighters of the Defence Forces, Civil Servants, the Judiciary and our Government, can be saved if His Excellency chooses to do the right thing. His Excellency, Cde Robert Gabriel Mugabe, has always said that if the people don't want him he will leave office. Now that they have spoken he must now ACCEPT the will of the people and resign. President Mugabe in his televised State of the Nation Address admitted to a number of [incidents of] patent disregard for the interests of the people and dereliction of duty. Surely after making such an admission, common sense dictates that it should have been followed by an apology and immediate resignation to save the legacy of our struggle. As promised in my last communication, I will be returning home as soon as the right conditions for security and stability prevail. I look forward to returning home soon and to join in the struggle for the economic revival of our country, which is so endowed with Agriculture, Industrial and Commerce, and Mining Opportunities and with a rich human resource bedrock to support our endeavours. My desire is to join all Zimbabweans in a NEW ERA where corruption, incompetency, dereliction of duty, laziness, and social and cultural decadency are not tolerated. In that new Zimbabwe it is important for everyone to join hands so that we rebuild this nation to its full glory. This is not a job for Zanu-PF alone but for all people of Zimbabwe. In my conversation with the president I told him that there are two options, that is (a) to co-operate in the current negotiations with comrades from the defence forces for a peaceful resolution of this crisis, which would result in the preservation of his legacy; (b) that if he continues to dig in, in defiance of the will of the people, he might suffer humiliation because definitely the will of the people will prevail against one person. He requested me to come to State House, and I replied that I was out of the country, and that he had already removed my status as the vice-president of the country, as such I had no status; however, I can only come at the invitation of my colleagues in the party and of the defence forces, when they feel that my security is guaranteed.

I am aware that Parliament intends to impeach the President. Parliament is the ultimate expression of the will of the people outside an election and in my view is expressing national sentiment by implementing the Impeachment Proceedings; therefore talks between myself and the President cannot supersede the expression and fundamental rights of fellow Zimbabweans. I am aware that the nation at large has been protesting against the incumbent and I believe they have a right to protest in terms of our constitution. I am also aware that the party has passed resolutions in terms of the party constitution. They have a right to do so. I will not stand in the way of the people and my party. I will go along with the wishes of my party and general population.

In conclusion, the destiny of our country is in the hands of our people, and His Excellency must heed the call of the people to resign.

God bless Zimbabwe.

Emmerson Dambudzo Mnangagwa

14

So near, yet so far

Two months after the fall of Robert Mugabe in November 2017, Jonathan Moyo, the former higher education minister and a close ally of Mugabe, gave an interview to the BBC on the events that led to Mugabe's ousting. Speaking from an undisclosed location, Moyo, who fled the country in November with his close friend Saviour Kasukuwere, the former local government minister, gave an account of the force used by the military in their intervention, which resulted in several deaths. He bluntly called the events a coup. Now standing on the other side of the fence, Moyo has been drawing attention to all the wrongs in Zimbabwe. It was not too long ago that Moyo turned a blind eye to human rights abuses and good governance violations that took place under the government of which he was part.

'Emmerson Mnangagwa and Constantino Chiwenga, they know only too well that they have come into power via the bullet and not the ballot. We have a constitution that the people of Zimbabwe made for themselves, and it has been broken and it has been broken via a coup. The army deployed itself in Zimbabwe when the constitution says only the president can deploy it,' Moyo told Zeinab Badawi on the BBC's *HARDtalk* programme.

His own account of how he escaped on the night of 14 November last year is unclear. In the BBC interview, he spoke of how 'angels' and

'God's people' had assisted him to evade the soldiers that raided his home. In her interview with the *Sunday Times*, Grace Mugabe said she sent two Toyota Land Cruisers to jointly rescue Moyo and Kasukuwere and their families. Eventually Moyo was able to leave the country and go into exile.

In view of his proximity to Mugabe, Moyo was one of 'the criminals surrounding the president' who were wanted by the military. On social media, pictures were widely shared of the early morning raid on Moyo's home in Borrowdale. Windows were broken, doors knocked down and clothes strewn on the floors as soldiers searched his house. Ironically, Moyo was a neighbour of Constantino Chiwenga, who lives in the affluent Borrowdale Brooke.

Forced to flee into self-imposed exile, Moyo is but a shadow of the once powerful politician. Often referred to simply as 'Prof', a reference to his political standing rather than any distinguished academic career, Moyo is many things to different people. It is precisely because of this that Moyo is often likened to a chameleon: he too has an uncanny ability to read the mood well and know when to change his colours.

While praise singers of Moyo are now few and far between, villagers in his rural home of Tsholotsho tell a different story of the man. It was he who erected tower lights in their village, got a bank to set up office there and oversaw the building of a Grain Marketing Board maize depot in the town. He also sought to build a football stadium, but that plan was resisted by some government officials. During the devastating floods that hit the area in 2013, Moyo was also at the forefront of relief efforts and donated food hampers and clothes to victims, while approaching businesses and government for support. The humanitarian assistance that Moyo provided shows a rare and otherwise lesser-known human side to him.

On the other hand, those who have crossed paths with him say that Moyo breathes politics and is a political schemer and *éminence grise*. Some in Zanu-PF have said he is a spy, a rabble-rouser, a divisive influence and that he was on a mission to destroy Zanu-PF from within. Media practitioners were always wary around him. The memories of the harsh media laws that he drew up in 2002 to restrict their work are still fresh in their minds.

I had almost an hour-long conversation with Moyo, alongside George Charamba, the permanent secretary of the Information Ministry, at the Holiday Inn hotel in Bulawayo in 2014, after a press briefing by finance minister Patrick Chinamasa. Top government officials were in Bulawayo to attend the annual Zimbabwe International Trade Fair held every April. Moyo at the time was the information minister. Our conversation was stimulating. Moyo and Charamba flatteringly suggested that my writing skills, then employed at the Johannesburg *Mail & Guardian*, could be better utilised at the Zimbabwean state-controlled media house. We all laughed heartily at the suggestion. There was no love lost between us.

Moyo has been a towering figure in Zimbabwe's political landscape for the last eighteen years, none more so than in the years following the elevation of Mnangagwa to the vice-presidency in December 2014. It was then that Moyo began to lead a spirited charge against Mnangagwa. The enmity between the two dates back as far as 2004, when Moyo convened a meeting at Dinyane High School in Tsholotsho to back Mnangagwa's campaign to become vice-president at the Zanu-PF party congress later that same year.

Mugabe, however, blocked Mnangagwa's rise and said the party would have a female candidate take over the vice-presidential position. Mugabe then turned against Moyo, whom he accused of plotting a coup against him, and sacked him. For his part, Mnangagwa was shunted off to the Rural and National Housing Ministry. It was then that Moyo's enmity against Mnangagwa began. Moyo felt that Mnangagwa had abandoned him during the Tsholotsho fiasco and had left him to take the fall alone for daring to champion his elevation to become vice-president.

Writing in the weekly *Zimbabwe Independent* newspaper, London-based political analyst Simukai Tinhu said Moyo had been an ally of Mnangagwa and masterminded his vice-presidential campaign. 'When this move was thwarted by Mugabe, Mnangagwa was simply slapped on the wrist and given a ministry at the backwaters of politics. However, Moyo, who had been given to think that Mnangagwa was powerful enough to protect him, was kicked out of the party. As a result, Moyo cannot forgive and forget the fact that the man that he had been working for not only failed to protect him, but is also said to have briefed against the professor when he apologised for his adventure against Mugabe. It is alleged that it was this subterfuge which has fuelled the animosity that today has become all too apparent. Indeed, Moyo can barely conceal his contempt for Mnangagwa and he has made it clear that he intends to make him a casualty of his politics.'

That fallout has meant that for years Moyo has been a man on a mission to avenge himself against Mnangagwa. He has carried with him a wound that has refused to heal.

On closer examination it is clear that the relationship between the two men was strained even as early as the mid-1980s, during the time of Gukurahundi. Mnangagwa was the state security minister at the time and wielded immense power. Moyo, on the other hand, was a victim and his family suffered the loss of their father during the killings. Moyo is clearly a man with scores to settle against Mnangagwa.

* * *

What gave the perfect cover for Moyo to plot his revenge against Mnangagwa was Zanu-PF's raging succession battle. But before Moyo could have the last laugh against Mnangagwa, he had inconveniently to work with him in order to deal with Joice Mujuru, who had caused Mnangagwa to be overlooked for the vice-presidential post at the December 2004 congress. United by a common enemy, Moyo and Mnangagwa worked hand in glove and successfully saw off Mujuru.

As a result Mnangagwa's supporters were in a celebratory mood, glad that Mujuru had been removed and their preferred candidate had inched a step closer to succeeding Mugabe.

While they were still holding their celebratory parade, Moyo struck, barely six months after Mujuru's ousting. He did so before an international audience and in front of BBC TV cameras. Speaking in a *HARDtalk* interview with Stephen Sackur, he boldly declared that Mnangagwa was no heir apparent of Mugabe but merely an appointee of the president. Mnangagwa's supporters, although livid, were slow to realise that Moyo was no longer an ally of their man. In the dark about his intentions, they had the rug quickly pulled from underneath their feet. Moyo became Mugabe's loudest cheerleader while publicly criticising Mnangagwa's supporters for seeking to push a succession agenda while the party leader was still alive. 'He is a vice-president of the country, one of the two appointed by the President to assist him to implement the President's agenda related to his pledges to the electorate … He is an appointed vice-president. The President did not appoint him so that he could succeed him. He appointed him so that he could assist him to implement the policy programme of the Government,' Moyo said before the BBC cameras.

When challenged on this by Sackur, Moyo did not budge. 'I repeat, he has been appointed to assist the President. As for these associations you are alleging, this is the stuff that you find in the newspapers. I want to repeat, this reference to him as the next President is yours, and it is a burden that you should unravel for yourself and not state as a fact,' he said.

These public remarks by Moyo removed the pretence that Zanu-PF was united as a party and crucially indicated that the gloves were off, as 'Prof' took on Mnangagwa, then still basking in the glory of his rise.

By refusing to be drawn into explaining the implications of Mnangagwa's appointment and what it meant in the political scheme of things, Moyo made many enemies for himself in Zanu-PF. State columnists were set on Moyo to denounce his anti-Mnangagwa position.

As tensions in Zanu-PF escalated between the opposing factions, George Charamba, writing under a pseudonym in the *Saturday Herald* in June 2017, went for the jugular, saying of Moyo: 'You have a personal tiff with this or that politician – your erstwhile ally in some past ventures – yet you seek to globalise that highly individual tiff; seek to make it a national issue. How and why were you allies in the past, how and why are you enemies in the present? Who asks: by what dimension does your tiff become national? Of national purport or concern? Need we then wonder why the political discourse in the run-up to elections is so poor, so sparse, with no apparent relief in sight? Inane, factually inaccurate postulates are credited with profound wonderment. You are an appointee in your party; you have no constituency, yet you think your viewpoint carries decisive weight in settling great questions of the day in your party! How so? Who asks: by what authority?'

Another state media columnist, Bishop Lazarus, questioned how and why Moyo had lost faith in Mnangagwa: 'Watching and listening from where I was, I kept asking myself: "Is this the same Prof Moyo, who was fired from Zanu-PF in 2004 following the Tsholotsho saga, where he was accused of being the architect of the plot to smuggle VP [Vice-President] Mnangagwa into power?" That Mnangagwa whom the professor thought could lead the country in 2004, isn't he still the same? What exactly has changed? Is it VP Mnangagwa who has changed or is it the professor?'

Dismissed from the Information Ministry by then, Moyo turned to Twitter to take on the state media columnists and rebut their claims. 'Charamba, oops Bishop Lazarus, I've said it before and I'll say it again: My support for Mnangagwa in 2004 was wrong,' he tweeted.

* * *

The fall of Mugabe in 2017 inevitably also ended Moyo's political career, which has seen a series of highs and lows over the past two decades. Widely viewed as a 'political turncoat', Moyo has oscillated between being a fierce critic of Mugabe and a fervent supporter. Increasingly influential as he was over the last ten years of Mugabe's rule, there is little doubt that if Moyo had not been by Mugabe's side, the president would have met his political end much sooner.

In 2000, Moyo emerged as the saviour of Mugabe's political career. It was at a time when the newly formed MDC party under Morgan Tsvangirai had made inroads among voters and had become a real challenge to Mugabe's continued rule. Mugabe was also smarting from the electorate's rejection by a referendum vote of a plan that would have further entrenched his executive powers. In search of a new saviour, he appointed Moyo to his 'technocrat' cabinet. Moyo was made information minister and soon draconian media laws, such as the Public Order and Security Act and the Access to Information and Protection of Privacy Act, were passed in 2002. Moyo swiftly moved to muzzle the press and churned out propaganda that there was a Western-sponsored regime-change agenda against Mugabe. According to *The Economist*, Eddison Zvobgo, a founder member of Zanu-PF and then chair of a parliamentary legal committee, called the new media laws 'the most calculated and determined assault' on Zimbabwe's constitutionally guaranteed liberties in the twenty-one years since independence.

Moyo stamped his personal mark on the Information Ministry, which before his appointment was a lacklustre government unit. It was moved to the Munhumutapa Building, the official offices of Mugabe, as Moyo insisted that he must be close to his boss. Moyo also banned the broadcasting of CNN and BBC and pushed for 100 per cent local content on TV and radio programming.

As a result of these efforts, the tide began to turn in favour of Mugabe, who had been on the brink of losing power to the upstart new political party, the MDC. Mugabe was beholden to Moyo. Of how close to losing power Mugabe had been, Moyo later wrote in an open letter in 2005 after Mugabe had fired him. According to this version,

Moyo had single-handedly saved Mugabe and Zanu-PF from imminent defeat.

The first sign of a fallout between Mugabe and Moyo occurred in 2005, after Moyo's decision to stand for the Tsholotsho constituency. The ruling party wanted to reserve the seat for a female candidate. The candidate that Moyo refused to give way to was Musa Mathema, then the wife of Cain Mathema, a former Bulawayo metropolitan governor. Moyo refused to step aside for Mathema. But this demand that he give way seems to have been a mere pretext, and the bid to get rid of him was linked to Moyo's campaigning for Mnangagwa at the 2004 meeting in Tsholotsho. Mugabe later claimed that Moyo was chief conspirator and had plotted a coup against him. He described Moyo as 'clever, but not wise'. Eventually Mugabe fired Moyo as information minister by means of a faxed message and he was given a few hours to leave his office. At the time of his dismissal, Moyo was booked in at a hotel in Bulawayo, and it was the hotel staff at reception who handed him his dismissal letter.

Once out of Zanu-PF, Moyo went on to contest the Tsholotsho seat as an independent candidate. He won. As an independent, Moyo received financial assistance from Mnangagwa, who gave him a black Toyota Surf to use on the campaign trail. During his time as an independent, Moyo claims, he, Mnangagwa and July Moyo formed the United People's Movement (UPM), a party meant to destabilise Zanu-PF. It was also around this time that Moyo began to develop links with the US embassy in Harare. US diplomatic cables, according to WikiLeaks, while describing Moyo as having had 'a checkered history' and being a 'one-time apologist for Mugabe', also detailed the conversations he was having with the US ambassador to Zimbabwe, Christopher Dell. The diplomatic cables said: 'He maintains good contacts across the political spectrum and he provides a window into Zanu-PF's internal politics.'

But after years of being out in the wilderness, which he himself described as a lonely experience, Moyo returned to the Zanu-PF fold at its congress in December 2009. 'His late daughter, Zanele Moyo, is partly the reason why he went back to Zanu-PF, because she told him that it made no sense that all his friends were in Zanu-PF yet he was an independent,' said a relative of his.

In part, Mugabe's acceptance of Moyo's return was influenced by the need to start preparing for elections in 2013. Mugabe had found himself in an uncomfortable power-sharing government with Morgan Tsvangirai after the flawed 2008 elections. Zanu-PF had also lost majority control of Parliament to the MDC, a loss that had never before happened in the country's history since independence in 1980. Mugabe needed a convincing victory in the upcoming elections in 2013, and he looked to Moyo for salvation. Mugabe's vulnerability enabled Moyo to organise a remarkable comeback into the very heart of Zanu-PF's affairs.

Within five years of his time in the wilderness, Moyo had clawed his way back into the upper echelons of power in Zanu-PF and the government, and also had the president's ear. He was credited for being the brains behind the economic blueprint released in September 2013, the Zimbabwe Agenda for Sustainable Socio-Economic Transformation, popularly referred to as Zim Asset. The policy was largely based on the revival of the key economic sectors of agriculture and mining and it promised to deliver two million jobs. For his efforts, Moyo was rewarded with the post of information minister. Yet again, for the second time, Moyo had rescued Mugabe.

* * *

Once allowed back into Mugabe's inner circle, Moyo positioned himself as the fiercest defender of Mugabe's stay in power. At the time that he was forced to flee for his life in November 2017, Moyo was one of the few men who had Mugabe's ear. It is also largely thought that he was the power behind Grace's ambitions for high office. A blossoming political relationship between the two began to emerge. Grace and Moyo had much in common, united initially by their hatred for Mnangagwa and their common interest in blocking his rise to become Mugabe's successor. Given her relative youthfulness and lack of political experience, it was in Grace's interest to support the continued stay of her husband in power or at least determine the outcome of the succession question in Zanu-PF in a way that would ultimately favour her. Grace's novelty as a political actor also meant that she could break all the conventional rules of politics when it came to settling Zanu-PF's succession issue. Grace shot from the hip: she insulted her opponents, and made unverified allegations of coups being organised secretly and of witchcraft attempts against her family. All of this was said in the public arena, instead of in hushed tones and behind closed doors. Grace's approach, first seen in her attacks against Joice Mujuru, was described by Moyo as the acts of a 'courageous person'. Emboldened by her success, she moved onto her next victim, Mnangagwa.

But why did Grace, after so many years of being a bystander of politics, suddenly experience a political awakening? Was there a schemer or political mastermind nearby who was whispering in her ear, urging her to become a politician in her own right and one day possibly president? Moyo has denied backing Grace Mugabe for high office. In April 2018, Moyo also told *The Standard*, a weekly newspaper, in an interview from exile that the claim that Grace was plotting to be the next president was 'a Lacoste fiction', stupid propaganda meant to 'sanitise the indefensible coup'.

All the same, Grace's support of Moyo was never in question: she defended him on numerous occasions during the Presidential Youth Interface rallies in 2017. When Moyo was alleged to have embezzled funds meant for institutions of higher learning, he denied any wrongdoing and his association with the Mugabes provided him with protection from the law enforcement authorities.

If Moyo rejected Mnangagwa as Mugabe's successor and denied supporting Grace's presidential ambitions, then whom did he support? Some political quarters have suggested that Moyo may even have harboured presidential ambitions of his own. The analyst Simukai Tinhu has remarked that at the zenith of his power, it would have been difficult to say that Moyo had further political ambitions. 'He is aware that he is not trusted by voters, but, most importantly, by political elites that are hesitant to align themselves too closely – a fatal political weakness if one wants to be a leader. Indeed, a part of his inevitable downfall is written in his propensity to make too many enemies and his inability to sustain the few political relationships that he has.'

In June 2017, Moyo hinted at the person he preferred to succeed Mugabe: Sydney Sekeramayi. 'The notion peddled by the so-called Team Lacoste that its leader [Mnangagwa] is the only one who is above or senior to everyone else below President Mugabe is false and that falsehood should stop. There are others that are senior to the leader of the so-called Team Lacoste. One of them, by way of an important example, is Sydney Sekeramayi whose loyalty to President Mugabe, the party and country, whose liberation credentials, experience, consensus style of leadership, stature, commitment to the nationalist project and humility, have no match. So there are others. In fact, I must add that even [Second] Vice-President Phelekezela Mphoko is senior to the leader of the so-called Team Lacoste.'

In the end, Moyo, who for years had enjoyed pulling the strings from behind the scenes, was unable to set up his preferred candidate, Sekeramayi, in Zanu-PF's succession race. Winning and losing are a deeply personal affair for Moyo. This is why he took on Zanu-PF in 2005, even against the advice of the party, to prove the point that he was a winner and would have the last laugh. His loss of the Tsholotsho seat in the 2013 elections was explained by the fact that he had been busy drafting the party's manifesto. Despite the loss at the polls, Moyo challenged his defeat in the courts.

The biggest blow for Moyo must be that he did not get his man, Mnangagwa, after plotting so long and so carefully against him. Now forced into exile, Moyo has again become a victim, while Mnangagwa once again has emerged powerful, after he was sworn in as president. For his role in supporting Grace and in helping lead the G40 faction, Moyo, alongside his associates Kasukuwere and Zhuwao, was fired from Zanu-PF when the Central Committee met on 19 November 2017 to recall Mugabe as party leader.

Perhaps the cold comfort that Moyo has while in exile is that he read the signs of the coup from far off and warned Mugabe about it during a Zanu-PF Politburo meeting in July 2017. During the meeting Moyo cast Mnangagwa as a schemer who was planning to topple Mugabe from power. But Mugabe failed to act on the information that he received.

With some hindsight, Moyo believes that Mugabe never imagined that the military would push him out. 'I think that's now for historians to unravel. But one unfortunate but true explanation is that President Mugabe never ever believed that Mnangagwa and Constantino Chiwenga would ever depose him in a military coup. President Mugabe was impervious to that possibility because he trusted these two men more than he trusted anyone else. The fact that Mnangagwa and Chiwenga, of all people, joined hands and used the military to depose him is something that I'm 100 per cent sure President Mugabe cannot understand, let alone believe, to this day, yet this is exactly what happened: Chiwenga conspired with Mnangagwa to oust President Mugabe in a military coup.'

In the wake of Mugabe's resignation on 21 November, Moyo took to Twitter to give what seemed to be his tribute and standing ovation to Mugabe: 'There'll never be anyone like Cde R.G. Mugabe. I'm grateful for the opportunity to have served my country under and with him. I'm proud that I stood with and by this iconic leader during the trying moments of the last days of his Presidency. Democracy requires politics to lead the gun!'

15

Life in exile

When I met Saviour Kasukuwere on a chilly morning in May 2018 at the InterContinental Hotel at O.R. Tambo International Airport in Johannesburg, his first words to me were 'I am alive; can you see that, my brother?' We hugged and exchanged handshakes in-between bouts of laughter.

Although he did not immediately explain why he felt the need to affirm that he is indeed alive, we both knew what he meant. When the military took over key institutions in Harare in November 2017, they also conducted predawn raids on the properties of the 'criminals' surrounding President Robert Mugabe. By criminals, the military meant the prominent members of the G40 faction, of which Kasukuwere was one. His home and those of Jonathan Moyo and Ignatius Chombo were raided by armed forces in the early hours of the morning on 15 November. Later, after Kasukuwere returned from South Africa to Zimbabwe, where he was charged with jumping the border, he submitted evidence of 113 bullet cartridges that his family had collected and kept after the army crackdown on his home in Helensvale. Ironically, his house overlooks that of Emmerson Mnangagwa in the same neighbourhood.

At the InterContinental Hotel, he tells me that the military action on his home was not 'a Mickey Mouse' event. Only God knows, he says, what the armed forces would have done had they captured him that night. 'When bullets are pumped into your house, it's not like somebody is sending you a bouquet of roses to wish you well. It meant much more. November is a time to look at and say, What does this mean for our nation? How can we make sure this kind of situation will never be repeated in our society? It's a traumatic experience and one does not want to take it lightly. It's an event that was very challenging, it was not expected, and it still leaves lots of bitterness.'

Kasukuwere survived after he hid in the basement of his house with his family and his friend Jonathan Moyo. His mansion was rumoured to have fifty-two rooms with bulletproof windows.

Once the local government minister and the national political commissar of Zanu-PF, Kasukuwere has been used to a life of privilege. It must have been hard for him to leave behind his feathered lifestyle and go into self-imposed exile in South Africa. Ironically, it was the same host country to which Emmerson Mnangagwa had fled weeks before him. At the time Kasukuwere had mocked the former vice-president, then on the run, for being a 'border jumper'. I ask him how he feels now that the 'border jumper' has become president. Kasukuwere brushes my question aside and says there was nothing to it; his jab at Mnangagwa had just been 'political banter'.

All the signs of Kasukuwere's new life on the road are there to see. Beside him, he has a small black suitcase and a black small bag. It is hard to imagine that just a few months previously, Kasukuwere had been in high office. Then, he was chauffeured in a luxury vehicle, attended to by aides and protected by bodyguards.

Almost as if reading my mind about this fall from grace, Kasukuwere says he has learned a lot during his time in exile, especially about how to take care of himself. He is dressed in a pair of white chinos, a white jacket and blue shirt. Being a sharp dresser has always been his style. 'Where I used to drive around with lots of security personnel, it's gone. I always used to tell people to budget and prepare for a rainy day and to never get used to having someone carrying your bags. You must be ready to carry your own bags left, right and centre. You must live the life of an ordinary person,' he says.

Getting down to the heart of the matter, I ask how he had not seen in advance that the military was coming for him. A former intelligence spy, he surely must have still had some links with the country's spooks and military structures and known what was about to happen. Besides, the telltale signs had been there all along to suggest that the patience of the armed forces was increasingly wearing thin.

But Kasukuwere, just like the Mugabes, admits that he never saw the possibility of the military stepping into the political fray. He bluntly sums it up as 'we underestimated them'. Much like the rest of the G40 faction, his focus was on the fierce political contest for power under way in Zanu-PF at the time. Their plan, it appears, was to deal such a decisive blow to the Lacoste faction that when the party's congress took place in December, their rivals would already have been floored. It almost worked with the firing of Mnangagwa by Mugabe, but the plan was then scuttled by the military action.

'In the party, Zanu-PF, naturally there was a contestation of power and President Mugabe had set a process in the party to move it to the next step,' he says. 'It [Zanu-PF] was going for a congress, for the purpose of identifying leadership and that is where new leaders were to be brought into the party. The process that had begun was such that any other person who wanted to lead [Zanu-PF], that was the opportune time to change the party leadership and this was about two or three weeks away from congress. One would not have foreseen a situation where the military would get involved in civilian affairs. This was a political party ... The military have a national responsibility to protect the borders of the country and not to direct or dictate the affairs of a given political party, so one would have expected that this would be respected. If the military had wanted to give advice to the party, it could have found avenues to do so.'

Kasukuwere believes that the military could have advised Zanu-PF in a much more 'organised' manner and not taken the drastic action it did to get the attention of the party leader, Mugabe. 'What happened was beyond what one would have expected in terms of giving advice to somebody. Their action resulted in the removal of Mugabe; in fact, it was a coup.'

After surviving the military assault on their home, Kasukuwere's wife and children found shelter at the Mugabes' Blue Roof mansion for a few days, together with Moyo's family. But Kasukuwere and Moyo themselves immediately left the property at daybreak after a subdued conversation with the Mugabes over the surprising events of the night. The group was in shock at what had happened.

I ask Kasukuwere for details about how exactly he left the country and who assisted him. But he refuses to shed light on this and instead refers to his helpers at the time as 'guardian angels'. 'It's very important to protect the guardian angels that assisted us; they did the best that they could to save life at that crucial time.'

* * *

Before Mugabe's fall, Kasukuwere's star had been steadily on the rise. In some political circles, it was not unusual to hear his name being bandied about as the dark horse in Zanu-PF's succession race. Fairly young, at forty-six years old, he was tipped by political observers as a potential successor, should Zanu-PF ever decide to throw its weight behind youthful leaders rather than the old-timers of the liberation war.

Kasukuwere's political career was an assured and comfortable one. As a leading member of the G40 faction, he had the ear of the president. This was one of the grievances raised by those who accused Mugabe of surrounding himself with a group of young people with no liberation credentials. Particularly scathing of this blossoming new romance were the war veterans.

In addition, Kasukuwere also held two important positions in government and in Zanu-PF. As the local government minister, he had oversight, among other things, of the urban centres. The major centres of Harare and Bulawayo had long been strongholds of the MDC. Kasukuwere's appointment by Mugabe to this portfolio in 2013 was largely seen as a commission to wrest control of the urban centres away from the MDC.

Nicknamed 'Tyson' because of his bulky frame, Kasukuwere is known to savour a fight. And true to his character, during his tenure as the local government minister, Kasukuwere clashed with various MDC-controlled city councils across the country. In Harare he crossed swords with local authorities over the appointment of a town clerk, and in Bulawayo he appointed a commission to conduct an inquiry into dodgy land deals arranged by the deputy mayor. The commission later recommended the deputy mayor's suspension from office but then the matter proceeded to the courts.

As national political commissar of Zanu-PF, Kasukuwere's work involved travelling to Zanu-PF's grassroots structures to rally support for the ruling party ahead of the 2018 elections. In the context of Zanu-PF's infighting, Kasukuwere held a key advantage on behalf of the G40 faction. He had direct responsibility for overseeing the elevation of people sympathetic to the G40 faction, at cell, district and provincial levels, while blocking or demoting those with links to the Lacoste faction. This simply showed how deep the divisions in Zanu-PF along factional lines had run.

The Lacoste faction was, however, able to fight back. It master-minded a surprise vote of no confidence across several party provinces, although Kasukuwere survived this attempt to push him out as national political commissar. This was largely because Mugabe shielded him from the embarrassment of being ousted.

Kasukuwere's protection from the top became apparent when Grace Mugabe came repeatedly to his defence at the Youth Interface rallies in 2017. On these occasions she often made a point of publicly declaring that Kasukuwere and Moyo would not go anywhere, despite votes of no confidence or even arrest by law enforcement agencies. Yet the extent to which Grace had accumulated power so that she could defend or judge, in public, both government and party officials and could circumvent state and party procedures appears lost on Kasukuwere. That Grace was on a path of growing power and influence is something he says he was unaware of.

'Did Grace want to be president of Zimbabwe?' I ask more pointedly.

'It never occurred to me that the First Lady wanted to be the president of Zimbabwe. On the contrary, you recall that at one of the last meetings of the Zanu-PF Women's League, she implored the president to name a successor, saying, Mr President, why don't you tell us who you prefer for us to start campaigning for that person? If she wanted to be president herself, she didn't tell me. I don't have any record of her saying, Can I become the president? If she held those ambitions, she never disclosed them to me because, as the national political commissar, I knew the thinking of the president in terms of how we should proceed and what the role of the masses and the membership of the party was in choosing the next leader of the party.'

Kasukuwere's political career came to a halt on 19 November 2017 when he was banned from being a party member by the Zanu-PF Central Committee. The final blow to his rising political career came with Mugabe's fall on 21 November 2017. However, Kasukuwere avoids describing his political career as over and refuses to disclose what his future political plans may involve. Instead, he says, his political life has 'taken a lull'. 'A lot has happened between November and now. I am out of the country and I am not playing any role in the politics of the country. Basically, I am not in the game. The politics to a large extent has taken itself away from me. Where I would spend the day dealing with politics on a daily basis, it's now a different ball game and I'm just an observer.'

* * *

After six months of being on the run and in self-imposed exile, Kasukuwere is tired of what he describes as the 'unpleasant life' of the refugee. His bank accounts in Zimbabwe were frozen in December 2017. He had already scaled down his business interests to focus to a large extent on politics.

So how is he surviving? 'Basically you have to survive from friends and help from family. The Zimbabwean bank account, even if you have it, what use is it to you when you are outside the country?' he says amid laughter.

Kasukuwere's determination to go back home is clear, despite the possibility of arrest. He speaks of the hardship of exile and the unpleasantness of being in an unfamiliar environment. 'Once you have left a nation, it's not easy; it's not pleasant at all. While we want to thank those who have provided us with shelter and offered us their hand, you don't expect in any society to be outside your own country. I think for the first time I have a better understanding and deeper knowledge of how citizens feel when they are forced out of their country. It is not a pleasant feeling at all. It's something that none of us must ever wish on anybody. Even if there are issues in one's country, we must learn to resolve them within our borders and find each other.'

I realise that separation from his wife and children has taken the heaviest toll on him. His children often ask him when he is coming back home – a question to which he could not give an answer for six months. 'Home is best. There is nothing that beats that feeling of just being in a familiar place, surrounded by your clansmen, in your own village and with your own people. Come what may, I am ready to face my accusers and have my day in court. Let me face what will come my way.'

For a man who played a central role in the ructions in Zanu-PF in 2017, Kasukuwere has no regrets nor does he slip into self-pity. 'There is nothing you can regret in life. It's the course of life. The nature of life is such that even if you regret, it's done. What do you regret? In terms of the position in the party, I was appointed national political commissar by President Mugabe. Your loyalty lies with your party and leadership before anything else. You must respect and support the leader of your country. In this case President Mugabe was not just the leader of Zanu-PF but of the country and, as a citizen of any nation, you are duty-bound to support and respect and not undermine the head of state.'

Gathering his thoughts about the new administration under Mnangagwa, Kasukuwere says that what he finds unfair is that the blame for Zimbabwe's failures has been heaped entirely on Mugabe. Collective decisions, he says, were made in the past by people some of whom are now to be found in the Mnangagwa government. 'I think that men and women in Zimbabwe need to have the integrity to accept collective responsibility, but to shift the blame for everything that happened in Zimbabwe on one man is totally unfair.'

In Kasukuwere's view, Mugabe's long reign brought both good and bad for the country. 'Mugabe led us for thirty-seven years. There were lots of challenges that every citizen can attest to, but there were lots of good things too. While there were bad things that happened over the years, there were good things over the same period of time. It's a balance sheet that we must analyse. We must have the courage to say to the people, We got it wrong and how do we correct it going forward?'

* * *

On 22 May 2018 Kasukuwere landed at the Robert Gabriel Mugabe International Airport in Harare, and so ended his six months and six days of self-imposed exile in South Africa. He was briefly detained at the airport by the police but was then released.

16

The hangman

If Robert Mugabe had hoped that the rope around his political neck could be loosened a little, to allow him some air to breathe, then Chris Mutsvangwa was the man who ensured that the very opposite happened. Inevitably, the more life was squeezed out of Mugabe, the more his wife and the G40 faction suffered.

On the eve of the street demonstrations on 18 November 2017, Mutsvangwa, the leader of the Zimbabwe National Liberation War Veterans Association, flew into Harare from Johannesburg and went straight into a press conference at the Rainbow Towers hotel. His audience consisted of local and foreign journalists covering the unfolding collapse of Mugabe's rule from the front lines.

'The game is up for Mugabe. It's done, it's finished,' Mutsvangwa told the media corps gathered at the hotel in downtown Harare. 'The generals have done a fantastic job. We want to restore our pride and [Saturday] is the day ... we can finish the job which the army started.'

In Mutsvangwa's view, the military had entered the fray to prevent Grace Mugabe from being elevated to higher office. Her unbridled ambitions were a factor in the tide that had swung so strongly against her husband. Her actions were detested by a large section of the public: they sympathised instead with Mnangagwa, who emerged as the hapless victim of a power-hungry woman. Mnangagwa had been insulted without end, poisoned, fired from government and Zanu-PF, and had recently been forced to flee the country to escape an assassination attempt.

Given the misery suffered by ordinary Zimbabweans under Mugabe's rule, the prospect of yet another Mugabe in charge after he was gone seemed unimaginable. Her sharp tongue and pushy behaviour were all criticised as unbefitting of a First Lady. If she could behave in this way with borrowed power, what was she capable of doing if she were to have absolute power as president?

Against this backdrop of the fears of ordinary Zimbabweans, it was easy for Mutsvangwa to call on the masses to march against Mugabe. It was a march against Mugabe in the present and also in the future. But far more importantly, the marches would allow the military, who were then under the glare of the world's attention, to retreat under the cover of the masses as they stepped out onto the streets to make their voices heard. The military's role, to scuttle an attempt at a power grab, had been fulfilled; it was now time to hand over to the people.

With Mugabe cornered and having no way out, Mutsvangwa's message was unmistakably loud and clear: he had to go. Mutsvangwa is notorious for being outspoken and for shooting from the hip and not taking any prisoners. The war veterans' leader urged ordinary Zimbabweans to turn up in their thousands in the street marches and at the rally to tell Mugabe, with one voice, that he must go. Mutsvangwa also dangled an irresistible invitation before them: the demonstrators would also march on State House. And if Mugabe still refused to step down, then the march would end up at his Blue Roof mansion in Borrowdale. The plush home of the Mugabes has an aura and mystique about it. Many Zimbabweans are aware of its extreme lavishness but have never had sight of it. Mutsvangwa's call was unprecedented in Zimbabwe's history.

It seemed unimaginable that the leader of the war veterans should be at the forefront of the crusade to oust Mugabe. In 2000, the war veterans were the fiercest defenders of Mugabe's rule as they spearheaded the land invasions. A pillar of support, the war veterans could neither see nor hear any evil when it came to the president. But in recent years, they had gradually changed their position. In July 2016 they turned around and told Mugabe that they had 'rejected him' and would not support his bid for the presidency in the 2018 elections. In large part, the fallout between Mugabe and the war veterans was fuelled by the G40 faction, which derided that constituency, convinced by demographic logic that the veterans were no longer necessary in the political matrix. It was a fatal miscalculation, the beginning of the end for Mugabe.

* * *

On the fourteenth floor of the Rainbow Towers, I meet Mutsvangwa for what is his first exclusive interview since his return to the country. A few weeks previously, he had slipped out unnoticed, and now he was back with a spring in his step and a large smile on his face. It was clear that for Mutsvangwa, there was simply no way Mugabe would survive this chapter of his life. Mugabe could try, but no matter how hard he tried, he would not succeed. With Mugabe about to be seen off into the political sunset, Mutsvangwa would have the last laugh. And, true to the adage, he that laughs last laughs the longest.

'As war veterans we change regimes, and just take a look and you will see what we did with Ian Smith's government and other Zanu-PF leaders,' Mutsvangwa boasts.

In the final two years of Mugabe's rule, as the president and the war veterans drew increasingly apart, Mugabe's relationship with Mutsvangwa had deteriorated sharply. In March 2016 Mugabe had fired him as the minister for war veterans, amid a concerted push by a rival faction to wrest control of the war veterans from him. Prior to his firing from government, he had been suspended by Zanu-PF for three years on grounds of 'gross misconduct and disloyalty'. After his dismissal, Mutsvangwa was quoted in a local daily newspaper,

NewsDay, as saying that he did not care because he preferred elected office rather than serving at the discretion of an individual. 'I neither care for that Politburo post, nor indeed for the ministerial appointment. So Norton constituency, yes; war veterans' chairmanship, yes; Politburo and Cabinet appointments – I don't really care. In fact, two days ago I asked His Excellency for the honour of dismissing me because I only came in to save the revolutionary ethos and not to be served ... I am in a different mould from the vapid and vacuous "Gang of Four" of Moyo, Saviour Kasukuwere and Zhuwao. They are clutching on the robes of Jiang Qing [Madame Mao] and Mao-era Gang of Four lunacy.'

At the time of his fallout with Mugabe, Grace had also upped the ante and publicly criticised Mutsvangwa and the war veterans on many occasions. This soured relations further. In his interview, Mutsvangwa's delight at the Mugabes' predicament was hard to conceal and in fact he made no effort to hide it. He called Grace a 'mad woman' for entertaining the thought that she could be president and succeed her ageing husband. More crucially, the military action had dealt a decisive blow to the G40 faction, with Moyo and Kasukuwere forced to flee into exile. Mutsvangwa cares little for Moyo, with whom he had several verbal showdowns during the last two years of Mugabe's rule. The clashes ranged from Moyo's liberation struggle credentials to his covert attempt to take control of state power through Grace. Mutsvangwa describes Moyo as a 'deserter', who left the liberation war in Mozambique for a feathered life abroad in the United States. Moyo, he says, had chosen to take up a career in a US-based organisation that was known to be a career path 'of American spooks'. Mutsvangwa was referring to the Ford Foundation.

This story of a war deserter who had become best friends with Mugabe is one that Mutsvangwa does not understand. Why did Mugabe befriend a person who was 'a sell-out' from the time of the liberation struggle and allowed him to 'worm his way up' in Zanu-PF and in government?

I ask Mutsvangwa to sum up what really went wrong with Mugabe's rule. He narrows it down to three key issues. 'Senility, a doting mad wife and an indulgence in spies,' is his curt response.

The military action, as far as Mutsvangwa is concerned, was linked to the succession question. Mugabe had been on the cusp of anointing his wife to take over power from him, without the consent of the kingmakers: the military. So intent was Mugabe in seeing through his personal plan that he fired his deputy, Emmerson Mnangagwa, who was the heir apparent.

'We are obviously delighted with the steps which our army took in correction of a situation where there was executive state capture, where State House was being captured by a coterie of young upstarts. They were using his [Mugabe's] wife, who is clinically mad, and any-one can see that. She has done outrageous things in South Africa of recent. This woman now thinks she can aspire to be president of the country because of her husband. A collection of utterly useless and incompetent criminal-minded young men had now accosted and asserted themselves with this woman so that they could take power,' he says, waving his hands about in the air.

As Mutsvangwa berated Grace and the G40 faction, the ruling par-ty's ten provinces were that day mobilising for a vote of no confidence against Mugabe. They wanted him recalled as the party leader and also to step down as the head of state. The provinces said he was incapa-citated by old age. Passing a vote of no confidence in Mugabe gave him a bitter taste of his own medicine. The Zanu-PF leader had over the years grown fond of using votes of no confidence to purge rivals from the ruling party. At the peak of his rule, in December 2014, he had used it brutally against Joice Mujuru and the faction she led at the time. Nearly two hundred allies of Mujuru were purged from the ruling party. A month before he was forced to step down, Mugabe had also fired several cabinet ministers linked to the Lacoste faction. Clearly, the G40 faction was on a warpath.

But soon the tables turned against him. 'The army stepped in to correct that situation, so I am very happy and we feel that we must now take the task from where the army left it,' Mutsvangwa says. 'They have done their job, it's a correction, but beyond that, the task belongs to the country to deal with this unsavoury situation which has developed. We as the war veterans are happy that everyone is now on the same page.'

Mutsvangwa has no kind words for Grace Mugabe. He saw her as a threat, as someone who had taken advantage of her 'senile' husband. 'All this is because he [Mugabe] is doting on a mad woman, who in turn doesn't want to change her physical address even if her husband dies. That physical address, State House, you go there because you are voted into power, and she went there by marriage and now she doesn't want to leave the place, even if the marriage certificate disappears with the death of her husband, she still wants to remain at State House,' he says.

'She is using every crook hanging on to her senile husband to abuse every rule in the country within the political party and everywhere to make sure that she doesn't change her address. This is madness that a country which aspires to be democratic, that somebody now says simply because my marriage certificate took me to State House, I should not leave State House. This is unacceptable and this is why we are very happy with what has happened.'

Of Grace Mugabe's allies, Mutsvangwa is just as scathing. He says his former schoolmate, Ignatius Chombo, the finance minister, was never a bright spark. He feigns surprise that such a man could have oversight of the Treasury and be tasked with turning around the country's economy. 'He [Chombo] couldn't pass his O-levels; he is dull and was now running around with the economy. There was simply no merit in these [cabinet] appointments. There is something corny that for thirteen years while he was the local government minister, Chombo had failed to complete any major project. No new airport, infrastructure, he had done nothing, let alone even constructed a multi-storey building. These are people who instead should have been taking care of cattle and chickens rather than being in cabinet.'

* * *

While he was in South Africa, it is likely that Mutsvangwa met with Mnangagwa. But he denies that any meeting ever took place when I put it to him. But as part of Mnangagwa's inner circle, Mutsvangwa's usefulness lay not only in his role of a hangman. His diplomatic background was also vital.

Mutsvangwa is an experienced diplomat. He was among the pioneer corps to be sent out of the country as its foreign representatives. He served in Brussels, Belgium, where he was accredited to the European Union. He also served at the United Nations in New York. In 1989 he was part of the team that observed independence elections in Namibia, which saw the victory of SWAPO. His last diplomatic posting was in China, where he served for four years from 2002 until 2006. There his brief was to drive Zimbabwe's Look East policy as part of the country's response to sanctions.

Mutsvangwa's responsibility in the twenty-one days of November was to mobilise support and to apprise regional leaders of developments on the ground. In an interview with the *Sunday Times* in March 2018, the Mugabes spoke of a 'third hand' that they suspect had been responsible for dissuading SADC leaders from coming to their rescue. Unbeknown to the couple holed up in their palatial home in Harare, Mutsvangwa was that 'third hand'. In a newspaper report, sources told *City Press* that a senior Zimbabwean diplomat had 'sensitised' regional governments 'to the idea and necessity of the coup' and 'received assurances that there would be no military intervention'. Mutsvangwa's brief was to neutralise the SADC regional leaders. His message to them was that the events in Zimbabwe were totally under control and there was no need for any intervention, military or otherwise.

'When I was in South Africa, I was thrilled by the reception that I got from there. Clearly, the Limpopo River doesn't exist between our two countries. We had meetings and they were very thrilled to have someone who understands what was happening,' he says. He also speaks of the close-knit ties that Zimbabwe had with Mozambique, Angola and Zambia – a hint about how far his diplomatic push had taken him.

In the end he has little doubt about who must lead Zimbabwe in a post-Mugabe era. 'Mnangagwa is the natural heir,' he says. 'The vice-president has impeccable credentials; we need to only go into the history of this man to trace his background.'

About a month after our interview, Mutsvangwa was appointed special adviser to President Mnangagwa in the first post-Mugabe cabinet.

17

The voice of the people

I did not have the chance to be part of the celebrations of what was a historic moment in Zimbabwe's history: the fall of Robert Mugabe. Even if I had wanted to, my profession as a journalist prevented me from sharing in the euphoria that swept across the country at the time. And so I emerged from those twenty-one days in November almost untouched by the dramatic events that had unfolded. I did not hug anyone on the street and I did not kiss any stranger in those moments of wild celebration. I did not pose for a photo with soldiers, who at the time were celebrated as heroes for their part in toppling Mugabe. I did not even have a picture taken of myself next to one of the army tanks that were stationed for three weeks outside the seat of power, the Munhumutapa Building, once Mugabe's stronghold.

With hindsight, I now have mixed feelings about the events of November and how I related to them. As a journalist, I have no doubt that I acquitted myself well and earned the praise of my colleagues, who relied on me as their eyes and ears for recording the events on the ground. I remember getting a call from the then editor of *Business Day*, Tim Cohen, who phoned to encourage me. 'Hang in there,' Cohen urged me. I also recall many conversations with my immediate boss, the editor of the *Sunday Times Business Times*, Ron Derby, who said,

'Your share capital has risen, mate.' It felt great to have the endorsement of some of my most senior colleagues.

The days were often spent running around to get a story for our titles. For about a week, the events in Zimbabwe were front-page news in *Business Day*. So important was the Zimbabwean story that I had to send a daily news diary to the news editors in the mornings, so as to ensure that nothing of importance slipped past the publication.

There was never time to rest and I regularly moved about with energy drinks in my bag in order to fight the exhaustion that crept in. It was perhaps this continuous state of being on the go that made it near impossible for me to have any feelings about the events that were taking place. I cannot recall any emotions. True, I was glad to see the back of Mugabe, but I was emotionally detached in comparison to ordinary citizens who were throwing street parties and playing their music loudly, glad that a new 'independence day' had arrived.

My evenings during that time were characterised by meeting journalists from international publications who had come to Harare from South Africa, Germany, the US, the UK and China. My contact details had been passed on to them by a friend of a friend who knew me and had recommended my work to them. For some of these journalists it was their first time in Harare. They had come into the country with just my name and trusted that I would be able to hand-hold them through the extremely fluid situation.

How, then, could I be like an ordinary Zimbabwean, when I had to keep my newspaper abreast of events with authoritative, insightful and on-the-ground coverage of developments in Zimbabwe?

* * *

On the day that the street marches were organised against Robert Mugabe, 18 November, at about 11 a.m., I walked out of the front door of our apartment, jumped into the car and headed off to Rainbow Towers to meet up with my colleague Mzilikazi wa Afrika. We had agreed the previous day that we would drive together to the Zimbabwe Grounds to attend the rally that had been called for by the war veterans. I scanned several news channels and social media platforms to gauge whether the call to turn out in numbers had been heeded. The torrent of messages on my phone, which was flooded with texts and video clips from contacts of the various sights and scenes, confirmed that there was indeed a wave of activity on the ground.

The 18th of November was a sort of 'D-Day' on which ordinary citizens would give the message 'Mugabe must go'. It would be the ultimate end of what had already been a most dramatic week. In that time, the military chief, Constantino Chiwenga, had warned Mugabe to stop his intraparty purges. The Zanu-PF Youth League had called his warning a bluff and Simon Khaya-Moyo, the Zanu-PF spokesperson, said the army chief's comments were treasonous. Seeing that their warnings were not being heeded, the army conducted an overnight raid against the G40 and soon announced that it was in charge of affairs. Meanwhile, Mugabe was under house arrest. But when pictures of Mugabe and Chiwenga smiling together at State House on 16 November were published in *The Herald*, those watching from the outside were baffled: Had a coup indeed occurred in Zimbabwe? And if it was a coup, then what kind was it? This was the question that lingered in the minds of those watching the events in Harare.

It was not until the street marches held on Saturday 18 November, exactly two weeks after Grace Mugabe was booed in Bulawayo, that ordinary citizens became participants in events that previously they had merely watched from the sidelines. Mnangagwa was to later tell Mugabe that 'the voice of the people is the voice of God'. In effect he was telling his former boss that the people no longer wanted him in office.

Having the support of the people had always been a key feature that Mugabe needed to legitimise his stay in power. Every now and again he would remind his listeners that the people wanted him in power. His rivals were also often reminded that they would have to go to the people first if they wanted a mandate to rule. In this way, Mugabe dared his rivals: would they be as popular as he was with the people?

Given that his legitimacy relied to a large extent on a show of popular support, it became very important for the choreographers of his ousting to give an opportunity to ordinary citizens to voice their position about the long-time leader. Perhaps out of self-blindness, Mugabe never believed that the thousands who turned out on the streets were genuine in calling for his removal from power. In a sign of denial, Mugabe claimed that those who marched against him were MDC supporters in Harare.

Later, the London *Financial Times* quoted George Charamba, his former spokesperson, who revealed that even as thousands of Zimbabweans marched on the streets, Mugabe was eating corn at home, presumably unbothered by the demands of the marchers. 'He was talking about his school days in the 1930s and anthropology and how it impacted on the colonial perception of Africans and their intellect,' said Charamba, who has been one of Mugabe's closest advisers for seventeen years. 'In the midst of such a highly charged intellectual conversation, we were munching corn; oh my God, he was very upbeat and chatty.'

Whether Mugabe accepted it or not, there was no denying that there was a huge showing by ordinary citizens on the streets. A South African friend who works at the South African embassy in Harare called me before I left home. As he was already in the city, he described the scenes before his eyes. 'The people really don't want Mugabe any more,' he said at the other end of the line. He had found it impossible to go to the grounds to attend the rally and so instead had decided to mill around the city centre and take in the sights.

Usually about a fifteen-minute drive, it took me nearly an hour that morning to get to the Rainbow Towers hotel in downtown Harare. Nothing had prepared me for what I was about to see on the way. It was observing ordinary citizens with the national flag draped around them and united in their call that Mugabe step aside that gave me the first indication of events. Taking in the sights of ordinary people laughing and car radios booming with the sounds of Jah Prayzah, I realised what a bittersweet moment this was for the country's citizens. Many were bitter, as under Mugabe Zimbabwe had become a laughing stock around the world. Wherever they went, Zimbabweans were forced to walk with their heads down and their shoulders drooped in shame. Now there was a chance to fix things, to make the country great again – if not for themselves, then for their children – and at least to have the opportunity to walk with heads held high. Outsiders struggled to understand this. I remember seeing reports from several foreign journalists who were quick to warn about the looming dangers that could come from citizens embracing the army. Personally, I was of the opinion that these kinds of reports ignored the public feelings at that time. It was akin to refusing to allow the citizens to enjoy their moment of liberation.

Our front-page story in the *Sunday Times*, which was carried the following morning, was aptly headlined 'The people have spoken'. I thought it reflected the prevailing mood on the streets; that the people had taken charge of affairs and had spoken out against Mugabe.

In my own little way, in order to try to at least be part of the events, I played a Bob Marley & the Wailers CD and hooted on the road, as I snaked my way through the slow-moving traffic towards the hotel. Although I had understood the march to have a serious intent, there was something carnivalesque and festive about the atmosphere. I wondered to myself if the sights and sounds on the streets mirrored the mood in 1980 when Zimbabwe gained independence from Britain and Bob Marley performed at the celebrations.

When I finally arrived at the hotel, we decided that instead of going to the sports grounds, which would have been impossible to do anyway, we would rather travel to State House. That was where the second leg of the march was proceeding. On the way we passed the

Zanu-PF headquarters. It is there, at the so-called 'Shake-Shake' building, that Mugabe had been hero-worshipped by party members and had handed out decisions that ended the political careers of so many Zanu-PF members, among them Emmerson Mnangagwa. Now, as we passed by, we saw a billboard outside with the face of Mugabe encouraging voter registration that had been torn up. Once a towering figure on Zimbabwe's political landscape, almost overnight Mugabe was being erased from the minds of citizens. We stopped and took pictures of this scene. Several young people were perched on the wall, waving T-shirts excitedly, in a gesture of victory that Mugabe had fallen.

The drive to State House was equally slow-going, owing to the sheer volume of people on the streets. 'We need to first pass by my home and pick up the madam,' I said to my colleague Wa Afrika. I had promised my wife to come back and pick her up, so that she could see for herself the events on the streets. With history unfolding before our eyes, I wanted to watch the celebrations alongside my wife and our five-month-old daughter.

When we finally got to State House, to our disappointment, the grounds were cordoned off by armed soldiers. None of the marchers were allowed to march right up to the gates of the large property, a symbol of the seat of power in Zimbabwe. The march was stopped along 7th Street by soldiers. We managed to park the vehicle in front of the police headquarters one road up from State House.

Just as everyone was contemplating the next move, a metallic-grey Toyota Land Cruiser pulled up at the gates. Inside the vehicle was Brigadier-General Douglas Nyikayaramba, with another army general whom I could not identify. Nyikayaramba had come to address the large crowd. With the military the heroes of the moment, the arrival of very senior army generals sent the crowd into a frenzy. Many tried to push their way up to them, and those close enough to Nyikayaramba knelt on their knees, thanking him on behalf of the rest of the crowd for their act of bravery against Mugabe.

Gesturing with his hands, Nyikayaramba asked the crowd to sit down on the tarmac so that he could address them. After what perhaps must have been a five-minute attempt to get everyone to calm down, Nyikayaramba spoke. By that time, I could no longer see where Wa Afrika was. The pushing and shoving of the crowd was intense. A sizeable number of local and foreign journalists close to the army general remained standing, much to the anger of the people seated on the tarmac. They could not see their beloved general as he spoke to them.

'Thank you for coming out in your numbers today, but unfortunately your journey has to end here. We will pass on the message that you were communicating by being out here on the streets, as well to our superiors. Now, please, could you all go back home. Thank you so much for your discipline and conduct and that there was no violence and looting of property today.'

But just as Nyikayaramba had given his few words, there was a commotion from a section of the crowd at the back. MDC party leader Morgan Tsvangirai was making his way to where the army generals were standing.

If Nyikayaramba's arrival had caused the crowd to become excited, then the arrival of Tsvangirai, hand in hand with his wife, Elizabeth Macheka, made them go wild. Tsvangirai first acknowledged the army generals and then greeted the people. It was not a party gathering that had brought them out onto the streets, he said, but a national event and so he would not chant any MDC slogans. In a red cap and dark blue shirt, Tsvangirai was a man at ease with large crowds of people. In his brief speech, he expressed his support for the military and urged his arch-enemy Mugabe to listen to the people and leave office. 'There is no way that Mugabe can continue to pretend that everything is normal. Mugabe must go,' Tsvangirai said. It was to be the last time that I saw Tsvangirai address the crowds. He died of cancer in February 2018.

For those few days in November 2017, Zimbabwe's opposition party, the MDC, briefly found its old spirit. The slogan 'Mugabe must go' had first been popularised by the MDC under Tsvangirai in 2000. That was when the party emerged as a potent challenge to Mugabe and Zanu-PF. The events of November 2017 gave the slogan, which had been on the decline over the years, a new lease of life. This time around, however, it was not just Mugabe who would have to leave. His wife, Grace, and their allies in the G40 faction would also have to go. They were all expelled from the party the following day. A Zanu-PF Central Committee meeting held the next day at the party headquarters also resolved to recall Mugabe as party leader. He was given twenty-four hours to hand in his resignation to the Speaker of Parliament or face impeachment proceedings. Mugabe was on his last legs and the world around him was quickly crumbling.

* * *

When Robert Mugabe did not meet the noon deadline given to him to resign from office, there appeared to be very few options available for him to resist. He had clearly become *persona non grata*, despite giving the impression of still being in charge and not being bothered by the mass turnout of marchers and demonstrators. In a televised speech on Sunday night, when it had largely been expected that he would resign, Mugabe instead said he would preside over the ruling party's congress in the first week of December.

Was Mugabe deluded about the extent of his control or was he simply out of his depth in understanding how far the political tide had turned against him? If he had doubts about the thousands of people who had turned out on the streets to protest against him, then the virtual absence of his cabinet when he called for a cabinet meeting on 21 November should have removed any doubts about where power now lay in the country. Only five cabinet ministers and the Attorney General, Prince Machaya, turned up for the meeting at State House.

Unwilling to take the chance that the impeachment motion in

Parliament against Mugabe might fail, senior officials in Zanu-PF began to open up lines of communication with the opposition to ensure that its MPs also backed the motion to impeach Mugabe. It is telling that the attempt to reach out to the MDC signalled that at the eleventh hour Zanu-PF remained unconvinced that it could assemble the parliamentary support needed to fire Mugabe. Although embattled, Mugabe, it seems, still had the support of legislators close to the fallen G40 faction, and they were wary of what their future would be without Mugabe at the helm. At least keeping Mugabe in power, by voting against the motion of no confidence, held out some guarantee.

Smelling blood, the MDC, according to a conversation I had with the party's then vice-president Nelson Chamisa, was keen for a written agreement with Zanu-PF on what it would get in return for supporting the impeachment motion. But the details of the arrangement remain sketchy.

When Parliament sat on 21 November 2017 at the Harare International Conference Centre, the impeachment motion represented a make-or-break situation. Failure to secure a majority vote in favour would be a huge embarrassment and could embolden Mugabe to continue digging in and refusing to give way. It was Monica Mutsvangwa, the wife of Chris Mutsvangwa, who first brought the impeachment motion before Parliament. The litany of charges included dereliction of duty: because of his old age, Mugabe always fell asleep at international gatherings, embarrassing the country as a result. Monica Mutsvangwa's call for Mugabe's impeachment was supported by other legislators from both Zanu-PF and the MDC. Listening to the parliamentary proceedings, I reminded myself of the remarkable about-turn: it would have been unimaginable a few weeks before that the same Zanu-PF, which then still sang Mugabe's praises, could call for his removal from office.

But could Mugabe, a master tactician and political survivor, have one last ace up his sleeve and possibly pull off a 'Houdini' and escape the process under way? It was widely thought at the time that the impeachment process could take weeks before it was finalised. The charges would first have to be read out against Mugabe and the accused would have to defend himself before a parliamentary committee. Only then would a determination be made and a vote taken.

This argument turned out to be nothing but hot air. Mugabe had reached the end of his political lifeline. It became clear that the tables had indeed turned when Happyton Bonyongwe, the justice minister, walked up to the Speaker of Parliament, Jacob Mudenda, and gave him a folder. Over the microphone in front of Mudenda, we overheard Mudenda question whether the contents inside were genuine.

At that point Chamisa, who later became Tsvangirai's successor, and about two other MDC MPs ran up to Mudenda and Bonyongwe at the podium. The MDC's worry was that Bonyongwe might bring a legal interdict to stop the parliamentary proceedings, a last-ditch attempt by the embattled Mugabe to buy a bit more time for himself.

With a group of journalists, I also ran up to where the Speaker of Parliament was standing so as to be within earshot of the conversation taking place. Chamisa then walked away from the Speaker, with both hands punching the air. A colleague who works for Bloomberg news agency said that Mugabe must have resigned. The sense that something momentous had just happened spread quickly among MPs. Mudenda asked for order in the House.

When the MPs finally settled down, Mudenda indicated that he had with him a letter that he had been given by Bonyongwe to read before Parliament. It was Mugabe's resignation letter.

'Following my verbal communication with the speaker of the National Assembly, at 13.53 hours, intimating my intention to resign as the president of the republic of Zimbabwe, I, Robert Gabriel Mugabe, in terms of section 96 of subsection 91 of the constitution of Zimbabwe hereby formally tender my resignation.'

* * *

Mugabe's fall was a cause for celebration by ordinary citizens, but as a journalist I had little time to celebrate. The news of his resignation had to be written up quickly for the following day's newspaper. And so, against a backdrop of wild celebrations in the streets of Harare, I got into my car, pulled out my laptop from my bag and began to write the biggest story of Zimbabwe's recent history: the fall of Robert Mugabe.

Below is the story that appeared on the front page of *Business Day* on 22 November 2017. It recounts the inglorious end of Mugabe, who had shown more than once his unwillingness to step down from office.

End of an era as Mugabe finally resigns
by Ray Ndlovu and Theto Mahlakoana
The end. Zimbabwe's longtime serving ruler, President Robert Mugabe, tendered his resignation from office on Tuesday to the speaker of Parliament, Jacob Mudenda, minutes before parliamentarians were about to vote for his impeachment. The resignation from office marks an end to Mugabe's 37-year rule, in which the strongman in his last days had his power usurped by the military, had street marches held against him and saw him rejected by Zanu-PF as party leader at the weekend.

Earlier in the week it had appeared as if Mr Mugabe would not step down from office as he had appeared on state television, saying he would preside over the affairs of Zanu-PF at its party congress next month.

Parliament emerged as the last push against Mugabe, who had come under increasing pressure to stand down. Parliament resumed sitting yesterday after a two-week break and a motion for Mugabe's impeachment was moved by Zanu-PF senator Monica Mutsvangwa.

In the motion, Mutsvangwa, the wife of fiery war veterans' leader Chris Mutsvangwa, laid charges of serious misconduct against Mugabe, failure to carry out his duties as prescribed under the country's constitution due to ill health, old age and physical and mental incapacitation, which had seen Mugabe incapable of a further stay in office. The motion was seconded by MDC legislator James Maridadi, who made an impassioned plea to legislators from Zanu-PF to vote out the aged leader. As the debate concluded over the motion and parliamentarians prepared to cast their votes, justice minister Happyton Bonyongwe approached the speaker of Parliament, Jacob Mudenda, with a letter. Mudenda asked for a moment to study the letter and then indicated that he had cancelled the proceedings of the joint sitting of the National Assembly and the Senate with an important announcement to make. 'Following my verbal communication with the speaker of the National Assembly, at 13.53 hours today, intimating my intention to resign as the president of the Republic of Zimbabwe, I, Robert Gabriel Mugabe, in terms of section 96 of subsection 91 of the constitution of Zimbabwe hereby formally tender my resignation,' Mudenda read. Jubilation broke out in the Harare International Conference Centre where parliamentarians had gathered, and the session of Parliament ended. Scenes of tears and MPs across the political divide hugging each other underscored the excitement.

Mudenda said an acting head of state would be named by the end of the day today. It is understood that Mugabe has already left the country, presumably for a Far Eastern destination. He normally frequents Singapore and Malaysia for health checks. Photos of his key strategist, Jonathan Moyo, surfaced on social media in which he was seen alongside Saviour Kasukuwere in a flight bound to Mozambique. Moyo took to his Twitter account to post a message that he was proud to have served under Mugabe's leadership.

Nelson Chamisa, one of the three deputies in the MDC, said it was the beginning of a new era and history had been rewritten.

David Coltart, the former education minister, said it was the 'end of a tyrannical' regime, and a long battle lay ahead for the country to lift itself up, after being reduced to a basket case as its economy tanked.

Mnangagwa had in the day issued a statement in which he warned Mugabe to either resign or face humiliation.

18

Meeting Mnangagwa

When I finally meet President Emmerson Mnangagwa, he gives off a hearty laugh and gestures towards his spokesperson, George Charamba, who is seated adjacent to him on the black leather sofa in his office. He light-heartedly corrects me and insists he was not the only victim of Grace Mugabe's volley of insults last year. I had asked him why he had kept quiet and remained composed for the duration of the nine Presidential Youth Interface rallies while Grace had several swings at him.

'I was not alone, he [Charamba] also kept quiet,' Mnangagwa says to me during the interview at his Munhumutapa offices in Harare.

Everyone in the office bursts out in laughter. There are five of us in the president's room: Mnangagwa; Charamba; Regis Chikowore, the presidential press secretary; Mzilikazi wa Afrika, my *Sunday Times* colleague; and me.

In July 2017 Charamba, who was also Mugabe's spokesperson, was given a tongue-lashing by Grace during a rally in Chinhoyi. He was made to stand in front of her as she rebuked him in public. Grace was angry that Charamba, as permanent secretary for the Information Ministry, had not given any coverage in the state media of her philanthropic work in Mazowe, where she ran an orphanage school. Instead, according to Grace, the state media, which fell under

175

Charamba's supervision, was fixated on giving coverage and attention to Mnangagwa and attacking his rivals.

'We came a long way together before I was what I am today,' said Grace at the Chinhoyi rally. 'I attended your wedding and am friends to some of your children, but you have never visited my projects in Mazowe. You spend a lot of time writing useless articles that do not bring about development. You are the presidential spokesperson, but you want to create a wedge between me and the president. You should know that the president and his wife are one thing, they are inseparable. You are the permanent secretary in the Ministry of Information. Why is it that there are some people who should always be written badly about? That must stop. You are always fighting with ministers. You should know that you are the permanent secretary and you are way below those ministers.'

Although Mnangagwa had deflected attention away from himself by way of a reminder that he was not Grace's only victim in the room, I sensed genuineness in Mnangagwa's laughter. After all, he is now Zimbabwe's Number 1, as the number plate on the official presidential Mercedes-Benz indicates. As the president now, it is easy for Mnangagwa to find the events of the previous year amusing. At the time, however, there was very little humour in being dressed down by Grace in public. In fact, some of his sympathisers thought that he had buckled and did not see anything golden about his silence.

I press Mnangagwa a bit more. 'What made you remain so composed in that way? Is it strength of character?'

'I congratulated them for insulting me,' he says and chuckles again.

I push him further, hopeful that he will open up a bit more. 'What was going through your mind as you listened to all those insults from Grace about you?'

'I knew it was false. So I could not feel guilty about false allegations. I was pitying them and said, What a fool of a person. How can a person go public on something which one tomorrow cannot substantiate? That is the comfort of one's conscience.'

'Looking back at the events of November and even before then, when you were being insulted, what do you now think of Grace?' I ask.

'I think that she was primed by some of my erstwhile colleagues in the G40 cabal,' he says. 'They were priming her to do things and she would take such information or agendas without interrogating the purpose. I think she was not as sophisticated as she thinks she is in what she was doing.'

'Has Grace ever extended any apology to you for the events of November and the insults she traded with you?'

'No, I am not aware of an apology. If she intends to do it, then it is still on the way, but so far no,' he says.

The interview with Mnangagwa at his Munhumutapa office in Harare had taken a wait of three days. On one of the days, we had dressed up after a call came through from our fixer that the president would meet us at his home and we would have a private dinner with him. But when no one came to pick us up at the rendezvous by 10.30 p.m., disappointed, we decided to call it a night. Securing an interview with a president is a difficult affair and usually a game of patience.

But this time, the confirmation that we had secured an interview came at around 5.30 p.m. from Regis Chikowore. Mnangagwa had just been in office for a hundred days and we were keen to find out from him how the journey had been. This is what we had told the Information Ministry officials when we met them earlier that afternoon to formally request an interview. The meeting was cordial and there was buy-in from Charamba and Chikowore. Expect a call later on, was Chikowore's parting shot.

When he called us that Friday afternoon to confirm that the interview was on, he said: 'You must be at the Munhumutapa offices at 7.30 a.m. tomorrow. Please be on time, as the president will see you at 8 a.m.'

And so promptly at 7.30 a.m. the next day we were seated in Chikowore's office. Usually civil servants in Zimbabwe do not report for work at weekends. But ever since Mnangagwa took power, a new work ethic developed; officials in Munhumutapa began to report to work at weekends. The security was expecting us, and when we arrived we were allowed entry without delay.

At about 7.50 a.m. we heard the sound of the presidential motorcade pulling up in the driveway. A stickler for time, Mnangagwa had arrived for his appointment.

'Let us go,' Chikowore said, and so we made our way to the wing of the Munhumutapa Building where the president's office is situated. Another security checkpoint and we completed our personal details in a logbook and were asked to leave our identity cards. A few steps up and we were led to a waiting room. By that time we were just by ourselves, as Chikowore had gone off.

In the waiting room, Wa Afrika and I chatted little, as we were unsure if there were any hidden cameras or listening devices. In silence, we went over our notes and the questions that we wanted to pose.

Chikowore, now accompanied by Charamba, joined us in the waiting room. Perhaps noticing that it was taking far longer than expected for us to reach the president, Charamba indicated that there was some delay related to the keys to the president's office. 'But you must know that the man you are about to meet is a stickler for time. He was here in good time and, because the office wasn't yet ready, he had to wait elsewhere.'

A few minutes later and someone enters the room and goes up to Charamba. In turn, he informs us that it is time to go. As we are led to the president's office, I notice that there are many people at work in an adjacent office. It is a weekend, I remind myself.

We are led through several rooms. In the last room before we are finally ushered into the president's office, there is a large framed picture of the president on the wall. 'Where was this taken and how old was the president?' we ask Charamba. He is unsure but promises to find out. At last we are told the president is ready to see us. We enter.

Mnangagwa is seated behind a large desk on which there are lots of folders and papers. He is signing several documents in front of him.

'Good morning, Your Excellency,' I say, wondering in my mind whether I should refer to him instead as Mr President. Mnangagwa looks up and extends his hand.

'Gentlemen, please take seats there,' he says as he points to the black leather sofas in the room. 'Please just give me a few moments to finish this,' he adds.

I ask for permission to take a few pictures of him while he is still seated behind his desk. Once done, he makes his way to us. The president is in an olive check blazer, a light blue shirt and olive pants. But before he takes his seat with us in the small meeting area in his office, Charamba tells him of our curiosity about his photo in the next-door room.

Mnangagwa walks out of his office to look at the photograph. While there I see him smile. He says it was taken a long time ago. While I struggle to make out the rest of what he says, my attention is drawn to the ease with which his staff relate to him. He laughs loudly with them, as he tells the story behind the photograph. He walks back to his office and Charamba closes the door behind him. A brief introduction is given by Charamba and then Mnangagwa smiles. 'All right, gentlemen, what is your problem?' the president says.

* * *

Soft-spoken and composed is how Mnangagwa comes across. Whenever he raises his voice, it is just to emphasise a point that he wants to make. His predecessor, Robert Mugabe, was a far more articulate and gifted orator than Mnangagwa, but whatever he lacks in articulacy and oratory, Mnangagwa makes up for with charm and wit.

Sitting in his presence, I find it is almost impossible to regard him as ruthless and cruel, as the man who various media reports allege was involved in the Gukurahundi massacres of the mid-1980s, when he was state security minister. He was born Dambudzo but gave himself the name 'Emmerson' after the American transcendentalist philosopher and poet Ralph Waldo Emerson.

Family members say his favourite pastime is fishing, but his first love is farming. Out in the fields is where he feels at home, rather than in the office and behind a desk.

Mnangagwa's charm extends to knowing when to make a joke, capturing his listener's attention and making his audience feel at ease. He speaks glowingly of his presidency as 'a new dispensation' and says his administration is committed to 'opening up' and that 'everyone must feel the freshness of the breeze from the new dispensation'. The irony appears lost on him that he has kept in place the bulk of the old guard in Zanu-PF by his side, even after his inauguration. These old placeholders still serve in his government in different portfolios.

But Mnangagwa's intention to open up has paid the most dividends abroad. There has been a thawing of relations with former colonial power Britain. Envoys from Harare and London have been criss-crossing the Atlantic as the two nations seek to restore relations. Harriett Baldwin, the UK's minister of state for Africa, met Mnangagwa in late February 2018, while his foreign minister, Sibusiso Moyo, was in Britain in April, among other things to seek support for Zimbabwe's return to the Commonwealth. At the height of the fallout with the UK, Mugabe had withdrawn Zimbabwe's membership from the Commonwealth in 2003.

Although I found it particularly interesting that Mnangagwa kept referring to the Harare administration that he heads as a 'new dispensation', I wondered if the term could also have something to do with his personal attempt to whitewash his dark past and emerge as the saviour of the country; or was it a genuine attempt to get the country thinking and looking forward?

Mnangagwa does seem to have little patience with the past, and several times in the interview when he spoke of the challenges that have put the country at a standstill, he emphasised the need to 'move on forward'. It is a theme that was also articulated during his inauguration speech on 24 November 2017 when he was sworn in and urged citizens to 'let bygones be bygones'. While in exile in South Africa, in the first press statement that he released, he also urged, 'Let us bury our differences and rebuild a new and prosperous Zimbabwe.'

In September 2018, Mnangagwa turns seventy-six. Because of his age, he has little time on his hands to dwell on the past. It took Mnangagwa ten years to become vice-president in December 2014, when Joice Mujuru fell by the wayside.

A family member close to him has described how since he has become president he seems to have a sense of urgency. 'It's like he feels that there is no time at all for anything. While we are happy about where he is, the reality is that he is also in the sunset years of his life.'

Perhaps compounding this new sense of urgency to get things done was his close shave with death when he survived a poisoning attempt in August 2017. Mnangagwa speaks candidly about that episode. 'Obviously if you poison somebody, it is not to improve his health. I'm sure it is to affect that person's health and I am grateful that friends of mine reacted so quickly that I was able to survive. I was quickly rushed from this country within hours to South Africa. But for part of the hours and days, I am not very clear about what happened.

'I know what precisely happened when I was taken to South Africa and I am very grateful for the professionalism of the team of doctors that attended me in South Africa. The poison in me was washed out, it took about six to eight days. I still have about 3 per cent of the poison and it's dormant, it doesn't affect me. I think so, that's what they say, I believe them. I don't get worried. So that's the situation about what happened. The poisoning could only have been done by those who do not want me or didn't want me. I don't think it was from somebody who liked me or a group of person who liked me. I think it was from colleagues who were worried about my being alive and where I was in terms of our politics.'

Does he think that there could be another attempt to poison him again?

'I'm not so sure that another circumstance of that nature can happen again. I'm a bit careful now, but they may still succeed, but I have no intention of also poisoning others. It's bad practice in my view, but I thank God that I have survived,' Mnangagwa says amid laughter.

While Mugabe has spoken about the 'betrayal' that he felt at being pushed out and replaced by his long-time protégé, for Mnangagwa the action that Mugabe took to fire him in November 2017 was a surprise. According to him, a one-sentence letter of dismissal was handed to him; there was no explanation whatsoever for the reasons behind his being axed. 'I never expected that President Robert Mugabe would ever fire me, because in my view I had full loyalty towards him. I was committed to my party, committed to my government, committed and loyal to my leader to the end. I also believe that he knew that I was loyal to him and I would never ever do anything against him. I was so surprised that on 6 November at about four o'clock I was served with the letter [to say] that you are fired with immediate effect. There were no reasons, just a sentence like that. I said, Well, if the boss says you are fired, you are fired.'

'But what did you feel when you got a one-sentence letter of dismissal, given your more than five decades of loyal service to Mugabe?' I ask.

'I felt it wasn't Mugabe doing it and that there were forces around him that forced him to do what he did. I believe that this is correct, because later on when I discussed with him, when I was in exile in South Africa, he said to me, Emmerson, come back, what are you doing where you are? We have a situation here in Zimbabwe and I want you here so we can solve it together.

'I said to him, But, *Shefu*, the people around you have caused me to leave the country. My life was in danger and they wanted to eliminate me. He said, No no no, come back here, come back here, come and see me at State House. So from that I could realise it. How could a

person within a week say "come back" after firing you with immediate effect? He sounded so sincere, like the man I knew, that this is
now Mugabe talking, the man I have worked for over fifty years under
him. I felt that what he did was not of his own volition, perhaps it was
beyond him.'

'But did you ever ask Mugabe for the reasons why he fired you?'

With a wave of his hand, Mnangagwa suggests it is unimportant
for him now to be furnished with reasons for his dismissal.

'No, I have never asked him why he fired me. It's not necessary, he
cannot rewrite the letter,' he says.

Once out of power, Mugabe was allowed to remain in the country.
Mnangagwa says he intends to show him kindness and give him the
respect he deserves.

In recounting his rise to power, it seems he wants to make it clear
that there never was any intention to humiliate Mugabe. 'The first thing
was that Zanu-PF, the party, the Central Committee on 19 November
last year reinstated me as vice-president of Zanu-PF. They expelled
the cabal which had surrounded the former president, Mugabe; they
were expelled. But they did not expel former president Mugabe as
the president of Zanu-PF, so I was reinstated as his vice-president,'
Mnangagwa says.

'So when I was inaugurated on 24 November last year, within the
party I was the vice-president, until we went to congress that was held
from 12 to 15 December last year where I was elected president. That's
when I took over as the leader of the party. But at the time that I
was inaugurated, I was inaugurated as the president of the Republic
of Zimbabwe. In the party, I was the vice-president, but then only
endorsed as president two weeks or so later by the extraordinary
congress of Zanu-PF, which he himself, Mugabe, had summoned and
convened. So that's what happened.'

With Mugabe fully out of the political picture, Mnangagwa wants
him to rest and says that this is what informed the decision to give
Mugabe a 'lucrative retirement package'. 'We want him to rest; he is a

founding father of our nation and our leader during the struggle. He is an icon of Pan-Africanism, so we want to preserve that legacy; he could have committed acts of commission or omission at the end. But if you look at his history, he deserves to be respected.'

Part of the retirement package includes a pension that is at the same level as the salary of a sitting president. Mugabe is also allowed the use of government vehicles, can be provided with state accommodation, and has his medical bills and household bills taken care of by the state. 'Where he has his own residence, we adopt that residence and we look after it. So it's quite lucrative; we believe that he will continue to live comfortably,' Mnangagwa says.

* * *

The rise of Mnangagwa to power as the third president of Zimbabwe over twenty-one days in November 2017 was an impressive feat. It must stroke his own ego and that of his staunchest supporters to have the pleasure of retelling with dramatic effect how events swung in Mnangagwa's favour and led to the grand finale when Robert Mugabe was finally elbowed out of power.

But Mnangagwa's swift rise must be set alongside the fact that his name had been in Zanu-PF's succession hat for a very long time. He was no political novice. He had acquitted himself in the liberation war and was a trained guerrilla commander who led the first group of trained guerrillas in 1964 across the Zambezi River into Southern Rhodesia. His military ties forged back then in the Bush War proved enduring and provided the bedrock of military support that eventually emerged in his corner in November 2017 at the height of Zanu-PF's succession fight.

Already in 2004, when six provincial chairpersons out of the ten provinces supported his bid to become vice-president, Mnangagwa showed that he was a man on the make. Although he was outfoxed at the eleventh hour by Mugabe, who opted to install a woman in his place, it was clear that Mnangagwa had a groundswell of popular support and was able to make inroads into the provincial structures.

With the advantage of hindsight, the scuttling of Mnangagwa's chances in 2004 was a Pyrrhic victory for Mugabe, as Mnangagwa was only delayed, not denied, in his bid to clinch the presidency one day. Many political rivals at the time erroneously wrote Mnangagwa off and went into celebration. But true to his nickname of 'Crocodile', he had briefly shown his jaws, though failed to catch his prey, and decided to go underwater and disappear from the public view.

To the undiscerning, it might have seemed at that time that Mnangagwa was no longer a force to reckon with. For four years between 2005 and 2009 he was shunted by Mugabe into the Cinderella Ministry of Rural Housing and Social Amenities. His stay there did not, however, represent a loss of power. In the 2008 elections Mugabe called upon Mnangagwa to become his election agent. It was a call of duty that appeared to serve Mugabe's interest. As the rural housing minister, Mnangagwa was involved in campaigning in the rural areas, the core of Zanu-PF's support base in the country. He therefore had in his hand the means by which Mugabe would claw his way back into power. The military reportedly launched 'Operation Mavhotera Papi?' (which means 'Operation Where Did You Vote?') in the rural areas in order to win votes for Mugabe. Mugabe now had a debt of gratitude owing to Mnangagwa for masterminding his continued stay in power.

Mnangagwa used that opening to worm his way back into Mugabe's good graces and once again earn his trust. In 2009, in the unity government with the MDC, Mnangagwa became the defence minister from 2009 to 2013, the first sign that he was emerging from 'underwater'. This powerful ministry enabled him to further strengthen his long-standing relationships with the military generals alongside whom he had fought during the Bush War.

But it was not until December 2014 that the crocodile fully emerged from underwater when he was appointed vice-president, thus becoming Zimbabwe's second most powerful man. His supporters were ecstatic and Mnangagwa was at one time called the 'Son of Man' by an ally and fellow cabinet minister, Josiah Hungwe.

Mnangagwa's rise to power undoubtedly owed much to planning, politicking, and the use of vast networks and a patronage system that supported him, but it is unlikely to have been hatched over just three weeks. Mnangagwa has been the heir apparent all his political life and had been waiting for his time to take over as president of Zimbabwe. Ultimately, his rise hinged on the one remarkable quality of his that may have made all the difference. That quality is patience. His supporters would call it stealth but, all the same, patience was the impression I had after meeting him: he is a man who is composed and in no hurry to get his way.

Mugabe had more than a dozen would-be successors during his political life. These included nationalist leaders such as Joshua Nkomo, the Zanu-PF founding member Edgar Tekere, and Vice-Presidents Simon Muzenda and Joice Mujuru. In the final years, Sydney Sekeramayi, the defence minister, emerged as another possible name, put forward by Jonathan Moyo. If Grace Mugabe's own ambitions are taken into account, then she too can be counted as a potential successor to her husband. But all of the would-be contenders stumbled as they were reaching their goal. All seemed to be dizzied by the fact that they had risen far up in the ranks and were near to power, only to take a misstep that proved fatal.

Mnangagwa, who has spent more than three-quarters of his life by Mugabe's side, had the luxury of watching all these would-be successors fall by the wayside. He learned from their mistakes, and it seems even when his own ambitions were thwarted, he knew he had to wait and not make a rash decision that in the end would prove costly. Mnangagwa may have got into office at the culmination of the events of three weeks, but his rise had in fact been a long-standing ambition that had taken him almost a lifetime to consummate.

19

Crocodile vs Cobra

It is 29 July 2018, the eve of the elections in Zimbabwe, and an unlikely person, the country's former president Robert Mugabe, is the centre of attention. Although he is not a contender in the following day's election, in which twenty-three candidates are vying for the office he occupied for thirty-seven years, cameras are snapping away as he sits slumped in a chair under a pagoda at his Blue Roof mansion in Harare. Zimbabweans are set to vote for candidates for president, Parliament and local government in the harmonised election.

Behind the ninety-four-year-old is a man-made lake that serves as a dramatic backdrop. In front of him are hundreds of microphones and mobile phones put on the table by about 300 journalists whom he has invited to his home. A metre away from where Mugabe sits is his wife, Grace, and their only daughter, Bona, who both look on. From time to time, Grace urges her husband to 'speak up' whenever his speech becomes inaudible. An aide also steps forward to help Mugabe sit upright when he sinks further into his chair. A cushion is put in place to prop up his back.

All the world's media outlets and leading news networks are here. Since Mugabe's fall from power, his family has not had such a large media contingent before them, and this is the first time an invitation has been extended to hundreds of journalists to the sprawling grounds of their home.

Their diminished power since his fall is evident: there was only one soldier and two policemen at the gate. In times past, armed soldiers would line up along the massive wall around the property. Now the Mugabes' security is largely composed of private individuals and people who used to work for him during his time in office and decided to stay on after his fall.

The previous day, election campaigning officially came to a close throughout the country. The rules of the Zimbabwe Electoral Commission (ZEC) – the organisation with oversight of the polls – prohibit election campaigning twenty-four hours before voting day.

As such, 28 July 2018 was the last day on the campaign trail for the fifty-five registered political parties taking part in the election. The two front-runners – tipped to be neck and neck in a poll by Afrobarometer – were Zanu-PF's Emmerson Mnangagwa and the MDC Alliance's Nelson Chamisa.

As we have already seen, Mnangagwa is nicknamed the Crocodile for his stealthy and patient demeanour. It is a character that puts him at odds with his rival Chamisa, who is nicknamed 'Cobra' for the speed at which he gets things done and for his sharp tongue. Notably, Chamisa took over the helm of the MDC Alliance within hours of Morgan Tsvangirai's death in February 2018. In an interview I had with him in March, Chamisa explained his sudden rise to power, almost ignoring the existing party structures, as necessary. 'Nature does not allow for a vacuum,' he said.

With their eyes on their first election contest, Mnangagwa and Chamisa each spent gruelling months on the campaign trail and criss-crossed the country in search of votes from the 5.6 million registered voters.

During that time, on 23 June, there was an attempt on Mnangagwa's life. A hand grenade was tossed by an unidentified person just as Mnangagwa stepped off the podium after addressing party supporters at a rally at White City Stadium in Bulawayo. Several senior Zanu-PF figures, including Vice-President Kembo Mohadi and party chairperson Oppah Muchinguri-Kashiri, were injured in the blast. Authorities confirmed that two people died from the explosion and forty-nine were injured. The police put out a reward of $100 000 for information that could assist with the arrest of those behind the act.

On his close shave with death, Mnangagwa said that although the grenade exploded a few inches away from him, he had survived because 'it is not my time'. 'Those who are trying [to kill me] are likely to go before me,' he said. 'It's my usual enemies … they are people outside of Bulawayo. They tried poisoning me in August last year, sending cyanide to my office, all these things I have been surviving.'

Unfazed, Mnangagwa continued on the election campaign trail until Zanu-PF's closing rally, at the 60 000-seater National Sports Stadium. The MDC Alliance held its final rally in an open space just behind the five-star Rainbow Towers hotel in downtown Harare known to its supporters as 'Freedom Square'.

Both parties put on an impressive show of numbers at their respective venues, with supporters turning out in their thousands clad in the party colours of yellow and green for Zanu-PF and blood red for the MDC Alliance. The slogan 'ED Pfee', which means 'ED is inside (in power)', was the rallying cry at the National Sports Stadium, while 'Chisa Mpama', which means 'a hot clap', echoed throughout the MDC Alliance rally.

In front of the crowds, the two political rivals, the Crocodile and the Cobra, made their last bids to woo voters. It was the final plea to the people to choose them to be the country's president for the next five years until 2023.

* * *

Although he is now an ordinary citizen, Mugabe waited until the eleventh hour on election eve before he made his views on the election known. It was typical Mugabe political brinkmanship. For years he has been accustomed to having the final word in Zanu-PF.

Again, he wanted his word to be final as the country went to polling stations the next day. Even in retirement, it seems Mugabe's old habits die hard.

Before the glare of the media, Mugabe declared that he would not support Zanu-PF in the election. Instead, he hinted that he would support Chamisa, the forty-year-old challenger facing off against the seventy-five-year-old incumbent.

'I cannot vote for those who tormented me, I can't,' Mugabe said. 'I will make my choice among the other twenty-two. It's a long list. I worked with Joice Mujuru and also Thokozani Khupe. There are other names I am reading for the first time. There is Nelson Chamisa. I have not worked with him. I have worked with his late leader, Morgan Tsvangirai, in our government of national unity, but I have not met him yet. He seems to be doing well, going by his rallies. Whoever wins, we wish them well.'

At his final rally the day before, Chamisa had said he welcomed every vote, even if it meant that the winning vote had to come from Mugabe. For the state media, which for weeks had been running reports that the Mugabes were funding Chamisa's election campaign, the comments from Chamisa and Mugabe's press briefing were used as confirmation that the two were working hand in glove.

Mugabe denied the funding claims when put to him by journalists. He insisted that his work with the opposition had only been with Tsvangirai, who has passed on. But for over two hours, in a live broadcast beamed around the world, Mugabe railed against Mnangagwa and his administration. He said that his former protégé 'was not always truthful' during the time that they worked together, he referred to his ousting as a coup, and he called for an end to the harassment of his family.

Although visibly frail, Mugabe hit the table with clenched fists several times to emphasise his points. 'Let tomorrow see people decide that there should be a big no to guns directing politics,' he said. 'Let tomorrow be the voice of the people saying this, that never again should there be an experience of a period where the army is used to thrust one person into power.'

While he may have put on a brave face for the TV cameras, it was difficult for Mugabe to mask his pain at not being on the ballot paper for the first time in thirty-eight years. 'That is the reality and it is painful, but that is it,' said Mugabe when asked how he felt about being absent from the race.

He also spoke with bitterness about the events that forced his resignation in November 2017 and denied that he had ever tried to put his wife forward as a future president. Instead, he said, his preference to succeed him had all along been 'Sydney Sekeramayi, the former defence minister and not ED'.

Adding to Mugabe's anger was his claim that Mnangagwa's administration had not yet paid him his pension eight months after his removal from power. He said it amounted to a paltry $467 000 and was not a windfall of $10 million as reported by the media. 'So after I had resigned, I had to go to the pension office to say, "What am I entitled to?" And they said, "OK, we will tell you what your entitlements are and the amount is a total of $467 000." Yes, can you imagine, that was the total amount. Some people are talking about $10 million and that I am entitled to two houses, one here in Zimbabwe and one elsewhere overseas.'

But Mnangagwa has insisted that his former boss has been given everything he needs to continue living a comfortable life. This includes a salary equivalent to that of a sitting president, medical aid, an official home and staff, all paid for by the state.

Perhaps aware that the bloodhounds were after his wife, Mugabe repeatedly asked that she be left alone and not be harassed by the state. A few hours after the press conference, a press aide, Jealousy Mawarire, who had coordinated the meeting, claimed that the last few remaining state security assigned to the Mugabes' home had been withdrawn. 'Bulbs, electricity switches and anything that made the house habitable was vandalised,' Mawarire said. 'The leader of the nine soldiers dumped keys to the house at Mugabe's reception and told the receptionist they had been ordered off the premises because of the press conference. Only two police officers remain.'

In response to Mugabe's comments about turning his back on Zanu-PF, that night a video was widely shared on social media platforms in which Mnangagwa said Mugabe was plotting a return to power using Chamisa. 'The choice is clear, you vote for Mugabe under the guise of Chamisa or you vote for a new Zimbabwe under my leadership,' he said.

* * *

Voting day in Zimbabwe went peacefully. The ZEC chairperson, Priscilla Chigumba, reported later that the turnout had been as high as 75 per cent, with no reported incidents of violence. Tragically, one person had died while waiting to vote.

The main contestants, Mnangagwa and Chamisa, cast their votes in their constituencies of Kwekwe and Kuwadzana. As had become familiar in the lead-up to the election, Chamisa was most buoyant about the outcome. 'I know that we are winning, we have already won this election,' he said after casting his ballot at Kuwadzana 1 Primary School in Harare. After he had cast his vote, Mnangagwa said he was pleased that the process had been peaceful and there had been no violence.

But beneath the fragile calm that prevailed on voting day was an undercurrent of tension that was coming to a slow boil. The MDC Alliance had not only got Mugabe's endorsement in the election – angering Harare's rulers – but it had also openly declared that it would not accept any result that did not confirm Chamisa as the winner of the presidential election.

Mugabe's endorsement of Chamisa was seen in some circles as a double-edged sword: would it be enough to swing remnants of the rural vote to Chamisa, or would it be a kiss of death? But while the impact of Mugabe's support is impossible to assess, the comments about refusing to accept the election results if they did not go Chamisa's way sowed the seeds of trouble.

South Africa's *Sunday Times* reported in its 29 July edition that the country's security forces were on high alert in the week leading to voting day. 'Members of the army who were on leave were recalled as the country's security structures are on high alert, in anticipation of post-election violence,' the report stated. 'Unnerving the country's security top brass are growing indications that the MDC Alliance may refuse to accept any presidential poll results which do not confirm Nelson Chamisa as the winner of the polls.'

The MDC Alliance had already held two street demonstrations to protest against the ZEC's management of the poll. Their grievances included frustration over not being allowed access to the ballot paper, not viewing the printing of the ballot paper, and also the design of the paper that saw Mnangagwa's name at the top of a second column. Their attempts to protest for a third time outside the offices of the ZEC were rejected by police.

For twenty years, Zimbabwe's opposition has found itself going into election contests in which they have strong doubts of a free and fair outcome. The dilemma it has repeatedly faced is whether to take part in the vote or to boycott it.

Chamisa, who has been a member of the MDC since the party's founding in September 1999, would have been familiar with this pattern. He has watched several times over Tsvangirai's shoulder – in 2002, 2008 and 2013 – when the presidency eluded his former leader.

Perhaps by openly declaring that it would not recognise anything other than a Chamisa victory even before the election got under way, the MDC Alliance was making an early attempt to question the legitimacy of the polls and put pressure on the authorities. It had an audience in the form of the several observer missions from the European Union, the Commonwealth, SADC and the African Union.

Its daring strategy went as far as announcing the winner of the presidential election before an official announcement was made. Tendai Biti, a co-leader of the alliance, did this at a press briefing at the MDC-T's headquarters the day after voting day. 'The results show beyond reasonable doubt that we have won and that the next president of Zimbabwe is Nelson Chamisa,' Biti declared. 'We are however seriously concerned about evidence of interference ... there is a deliberate delay in announcing the results. This delay is totally unacceptable.'

Because of his comments, Biti was wanted by the police. The sole mandate of announcing a winner lies with the electoral commission and Biti's comments were seen as responsible for inciting the public violence that broke out later. He fled to Zambia, where he applied for political asylum. After his application was turned down by Zambian authorities and he was sent back to Zimbabwe, he appeared in court to face the charges.

Meanwhile, the official results for the parliamentary election indicated that Zanu-PF had won a two-thirds majority. The MDC Alliance had kept its majority in the urban areas, while Zanu-PF had retained its stranglehold in the rural areas. With 70 per cent of Zimbabwe's population in the rural areas and the rest in urban areas, the alliance's hope of controlling the 210 seats in Parliament slipped through its hands. There was to be no repeat of the phenomenon of 2008, when the opposition broke the vice-like grip of Zanu-PF and controlled Parliament for the first time.

The results for the presidential election were slower to emerge, something that did not sit well with the opposition. At around midday on 1 August, MDC supporters gathered outside the Rainbow Towers where they wanted access to the ZEC's national command centre. But riot police barred them from entering the premises. The demonstrators regrouped around 2 p.m., armed with sticks and stones, barricading roads leading to the hotel. At the nearby Zanu-PF headquarters, a billboard of Mnangagwa was vandalised. The army responded by beating demonstrators with whips and firing live ammunition at civilians. Six people were killed and twenty-seven people were arrested by police.

Mnangagwa blamed the MDC Alliance for provoking the response from the security forces. He said he would set up an independent commission of inquiry to investigate the deployment of the military on citizens.

The protests and the deaths of civilians put a damper on the peaceful election. Even as the country waited for the results of the presidential election, which came in the early hours of Friday 3 August, army helicopters hovered over the capital, shops in the city centre closed early, and people knocked off from work early and most stayed indoors.

* * *

Early on Friday morning, Chigumba announced the final presidential results. Mnangagwa was declared the winner of the poll with 50.8 per cent of the vote to Chamisa's 44.3 per cent. The rural vote had swung the win in Mnangagwa's favour, while his rival had received the bulk of his support from the urban areas.

As expected, the MDC Alliance rejected the results of the presidential elections. It called for a press briefing at the Bronte Hotel to make its position known to the media. But before the event could even get under way, police in full riot gear tried to break up the meeting – which was seen as a political gathering. Media watchdog MISA Zimbabwe said the police action 'cast the country in a bad light locally and internationally'. For Chamisa, the episode provided him with more political ammunition. 'It simply shows Mnangagwa had something to hide,' he said.

In his first address after the results announcement, Chamisa was combative. 'We have so much evidence and we are going to be challenging the result,' he said. 'We actually got a majority vote in the presidential election, had it not been for the manipulation. The MDC

Alliance structures are working to roll out a programme of action to protect the will of the people.'

The evidence that the alliance claimed to have included eyewitness accounts, videos of unsealed ballot boxes being taken to unknown locations and proof that V11 forms – posted outside a polling station to show the results when vote-counting finishes – were manipulated.

But just a few blocks away, while the defeated Cobra talked war, the victorious Crocodile pledged peace at State House. 'Our democratic process for the first time was open to the world like never before. The campaign was hard-fought and at times competitive, as it should be,' said Mnangagwa, adding that Chamisa had a 'crucial role' to play in the country's future.

Soon afterwards, questions were raised about who was responsible for the crackdown on protesters. A Bloomberg news report published on 7 August 2018 claimed that army commander Valerio Sibanda was not aware of who had ordered the deployment of the army onto Harare's streets. The report, which quoted unnamed sources, said: 'General Philip Valerio Sibanda asked for an explanation from President-elect Emmerson Mnangagwa, his advisers and intelligence chiefs of the events on 1 August that left six people dead in the capital, Harare, and raised questions about who controls the security forces.' In the same report, Sibusiso Moyo, the foreign affairs minister who had risen to prominence for his address on state TV in the early hours of 15 November 2017, said the aggressors were not soldiers. 'We're witnessing what are purported soldiers, but they're not soldiers, and we're very busy investigating this,' he said. As reports emerged of widespread post-election violence that had spilled into some of Harare's townships, army spokesperson Overson Mugwisi said those involved were not members of the army. 'The Zimbabwe Defence Forces has not deployed soldiers in any residential area to beat people up at night or any time of day,' he said. 'If there are individuals masquerading as our members committing crime, these might be criminals bent on tarnishing the image of the Zimbabwe Defence Forces.' This lack of clarity adds to the need for an independent commission of inquiry into the events of 1 August.

* * *

A week after the election results were announced, Chamisa's legal team filed the party's court challenge of the presidential results at the Constitutional Court. The alliance enlisted two top legal minds from South Africa, Advocates Tembeka Ngcukaitobi and Dali Mpofu, to challenge Mnangagwa's win. The court challenge, filed at the eleventh hour, led to the cancellation of Mnangagwa's inauguration ceremony pending the outcome of the court case. At least fifteen heads of state from the region had initially confirmed their attendance to the ceremony.

In an interview for *Sunday Times*, Ngcukaitobi told me that he had taken up the case as the MDC Alliance's challenge 'looks solid' and it was 'entitled to proper constitutional arguments to advance its cause'.

A full bench of nine judges led by Chief Justice Luke Malaba was set to make a ruling on the case within fourteen days. Legal watchdogs said the highest court in the land had one of several options. It could invalidate the election, in which case a fresh election must be held within sixty days; it could order a recount of votes; or it could order a run-off if it found that none of the candidates had more than 50 per cent of the vote. As this book was about to go to print, the country's top court had not yet made its ruling. Zanu-PF had only just filed its opposing papers after two public holidays in mid-August, Heroes' Day and Defence Forces Day. It asked that the Constitutional Court throw out the case on the grounds of technicality, stemming from the failure by the MDC Alliance to meet the deadline to make its submission.

In three weeks, the fight between Mnangagwa and Chamisa had moved from the ballot box to the streets and finally into the court-

'It is not for the court to decide elections, it is the people,' said Malaba. 'It is the duty of the court to strive in the public interest to sustain that which the people have expressed their will in. Therefore this application ought to be dismissed with costs ... Emmerson Dambudzo Mnangagwa is duly declared the winner of the presidential election held on the 30th of July 2018.'

Chamisa would later tell a news conference the following day at the party's headquarters in Harare that he respectfully disagreed with the top court's ruling. He also spurned an offer of reconciliation from Mnangagwa. 'The legal doors are not the only ones available, political doors are going to be opened,' he said. 'This includes the right to peaceful demonstrations. This will be done in a very short space of time.'

On 26 August, the National Sports Stadium was filled to capacity as thousands of Zimbabweans attended Mnangagwa's inauguration ceremony. The Crocodile's hold on power had only been delayed, but was not denied. Several heads of state were in attendance, including South Africa's Cyril Ramaphosa, Rwanda's Paul Kagame, Zambia's Edgar Lungu and the Democratic Republic of Congo's Joseph Kabila, as well as several former heads of state. The mood was celebratory.

Before he gave his inauguration speech, Mnangagwa read a letter from Robert Mugabe, whom he had invited to the ceremony but who did not attend. The Mugabes said that they were unwell. 'Hearty congratulations,' Mugabe wrote to Mnangagwa – a message that received a thunderous applause from the packed stadium.

As he took up the role of running Zimbabwe for the next five years, Mnangagwa was once again reconciliatory.

'What unites us,' he declared, 'is far greater than what divides us.'

20

What next for Zimbabwe?

The victory of Emmerson Mnangagwa in the Zanu-PF succession race in 2017 was not just a personal triumph against rivals in the ruling party who intended to put an end to his long political career. It was a victory that had far greater importance and in essence cascaded beyond Mnangagwa as an individual. The triumph of November 2017 symbolised a victory for the military. The military had once again confirmed its status as the ultimate kingmakers in Zimbabwe's politics.

In modern-day Zimbabwe, the military had opted to play a behind-the-scenes role in influencing the direction of the country's politics. But it increasingly lost this clout as the succession question raged in Zanu-PF. A new dynamic was introduced when much younger leaders entered the scene, intent on destroying its role and significance in determining the country's future.

Before the 2018 elections, there had been widespread concerns that the military would be involved in influencing the outcome. Army spokesperson Overson Mugwisi said, however, that the army would have no 'direct role' in the elections, and that it would merely support the police in maintaining law and order before, during and after the poll. In the end, the army's heavy-handed response to opposition protestors resulted in six deaths. Mnangagwa pledged to set up an independent commission of inquiry into these events.

Under Mnangagwa, himself a military man, Zimbabwe is likely to see the military become more visible in influencing civilian matters. In his first cabinet, three top military men who had played different roles in the fall of Mugabe took up key positions in government. For instance, Mnangagwa's deputy, Constantino Chiwenga, is a former military general and is likely to be the next in line to take over after him.

Whereas Mugabe lost support both within the region and internationally, Mnangagwa has shown himself keen to open up lines of communication with the community of global citizens. This approach is likely to result in Zimbabwe finding its place in the wider world. The international community, nevertheless, will embrace the new rulers in Harare cautiously and watch them closely. The administration will be judged not by what it says but by how much it walks the talk.

The reinvigoration of the military also places a renewed demand on the country's opposition parties to work together and put together a united front. Its fragmentation can only inflict further damage on the country.

The process of rebuilding Zimbabwe is under way and citizens want to see quick change. In this regard, there will inevitably be disappointment as change is likely to be painfully slow. But there is goodwill everywhere and a desire to see Zimbabwe and its citizens get back on their feet.

The onus rests on Zimbabwe, and particularly on its leadership, to make the necessary changes that will turn the country once more into the breadbasket of the region and the jewel of Africa.

Index